LANDSCAPES OF
Mallorca

a countryside guide

Valerie Crespí-Green

D1326750

SUNFLOWER
BOOKS

First published 1984 by
Sunflower Books
12 Kendrick Mews
London SW7 3HG, UK

ISBN: 0-9506942-5-8

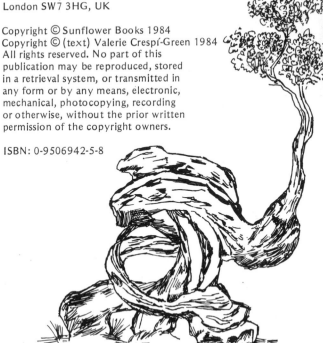

IMPORTANT NOTE TO THE READER

I have tried to ensure that the descriptions and maps in this book
are error-free at press date. The book will be up-dated, where
necessary, whenever future printings permit. It will be very helpful
to me to receive your comments (sent in care of the publishers,
please), for the up-dating of future printings.

I also rely on walkers to take along a good supply of common
sense — as well as this book — on their rambles. Conditions change
fairly quickly on Mallorca: storm damage can make a walk unsafe,
or a route currently open to walkers could be enclosed in private
land. If a route is not as I outline it, and your way ahead is not
secure, return to the point of departure. **Do not attempt to complete
a walk under hazardous conditions.** Please read carefully the notes
on pages 58 to 65 and make your walks *safely*, while at the same
time respecting the privacy of Mallorca's farmlands.

Drawings by Katharina Kelly
Maps by Pat Underwood and Katharina Kelly
Photographs by John Underwood
Typeset by Allset Composition, London
Colour origination by Columbia Offset (UK) Ltd
Printed and bound in the UK by A Wheaton and Co Ltd, Exeter

Contents

WALKS ON THE POLLENSA—ARTA AXIS

Foreword

by Air Vice Marshall Sir Bernard Chacksfield, K.B.E., C.B., R.A.F. (Retired); Member World Scout Committee 1972-1978; Chief Commissioner of Scouts for England 1968-1980

Mallorca is world-renowned as an ideal holiday centre, and I personally have enjoyed discovering the island over many years. Sunshine and beaches are the first delights that spring to mind when thinking of the island. Less well known to many visitors is the beauty of the mountains — amongst which are some of the loveliest walks in the world.

Valerie has produced an excellent book, based upon her personal exploration on many walks over the island. It will help walkers, bird-watchers and other lovers of nature to increase their enjoyment of this lovely island and will contribute to the pleasure of *all* holiday-makers who can use it to discover new island landscapes. I can thoroughly recommend it.

Preface

When you think of Mallorca, do you imagine a typical holiday island — hotels and souvenir shops strung out along busy esplanades... bars advertising 'English Fish and Chips' and 'Tea Like Mum Makes'... a multitude of night clubs and discos advertising *flamenco* shows on large and gaudy posters? Do you think this is Mallorca?

I hope not.

Of course, the hotel-crowded esplanades *do* exist, but beyond the tourist centres, an exciting and altogether different Mallorca awaits your discovery. And with this new addition to the 'Landscapes' series, I hope to help you to find it.

The book is divided into three main parts — **touring, picnicking** and **walking**, each with its own introduction. *Do* take a look at each introductory section, even if you think it may not apply to your holiday plans. You may find something of interest, because each section of the book has been written with one aim in view — to help you discover the 'hidden' Mallorca that most tourists never see.

Motorists will find that the ten car tours cover more than enough territory for the average visit. The touring map has purposely been kept to a compact, easy-to-use format. It is up-to-date and contains information not found on other maps — for instance, where some roads are now closed to motorists, picnic sites with tables, and the location of walks along the route of your car tour.

Picnickers can travel by private or public transport to all the picnic spots — some of them chosen for their delightful surroundings, others for their far-reaching views. *All* of the picnic spots have one thing in common: you won't have to walk very far from your transport to reach them.

Walkers of all ages and abilities will enjoy discovering the island's hidden landscapes as they cross an incredible variety of terrain — some spectacular, some serene. For beginners, there are easy strolls along flat tracks by the coast (for instance, Walk 23) and others (like Short walk 17) on delightful country lanes. Hardy walkers can tackle more challenging terrain to *miradors* only accessible on foot, and experts can scale mountain peaks or descend into the depths of the Pareis gorge.

7

Acknowledgements

I am extremely grateful for the invaluable help of the following:

For guiding: Mauricio Espinar, without whose extensive knowledge and experience this book could not have been written.

For permission to adapt their maps: The Servicio Geográfico del Ejercito, Madrid.

For checking the walks: David and Sally Murch, Clive Scott, John and Pat Underwood.

Finally, my most grateful thanks also to Maria-José and Francisco Merchán, for their valuable assistance in taking notes and giving me a rest from driving; and special thanks to Sharon Ranero for accompanying me on some of the walks.

Books and maps

Of the many books that have been written about the island, I recommend Ann Hoffmann's *Majorca* (David & Charles, 1978). It includes a bit of everything — history, culture, traditions, etc.

The island's natural history is well documented in James Parrack's *The Naturalist in Majorca* (David & Charles, 1973). *Plants of the Balerics*, by A Bonner (Editorial Moll, 1976) can be found in some shops on Mallorca itself.

For bird-lovers there is an excellent small book by Eddie Watkinson, *A Guide to Bird Watching on Mallorca*. Unfortunately, this book is not widely available, but can usually be found in shops in Pollensa and Puerto de Pollensa.

No maps of the island can claim to be correct in every detail, unfortunately. The map in this book should be more

than adequate for most touring needs, and it is the *only* map which shows the location of picnic areas and walks. However, if you require a map showing all the island roads, the Firestone map (available at hotels, kiosks and petrol stations) is highly recommended.

All the other information you need to get the most out of your holiday is available free from the Tourist Information Office on the Avenida Rey Jaime III and at various other tourist information kiosks in Palma and other resorts around the island.

Getting about

There is no doubt that a **hired car** is the most convenient way of getting about Mallorca, and car rental on the island is good value. Be sure to 'shop around' amongst the many car-hire firms (where English is spoken generally); the prices can vary by up to perhaps 40 per cent!

The second most flexible form of transport is to hire a **taxi**, and, especially if three or four people are sharing the cost, this becomes an attractive idea. If you're making a taxi journey outside the city centre (an un-metred journey), do agree on the price *before* setting out; all taxi-drivers should carry an official price list.

Coach tours are the most popular way of seeing Mallorca, and veritable convoys of tourist-loaded coaches converge onto the roads during the summer season, much to the frustration of the local drivers (and tourists in hired cars). However, you can get to know the island comfortably in this way, before embarking on your own adventures.

The most economical way of getting about is by local transport — hourly **train** services on the Palma—Inca line; the 'wild-west' **narrow-gauge railway** between Palma and Soller; the **tram** between Puerto de Soller and Soller, and finally the local **bus** network. All these public transport systems are economical, reliable — and much more fun! The Soller train is one of the island's tourist attractions. But the train between Palma and Inca is also amusing: the run is a flat one across the plain and the train hurtles along like a 'blue bullet'. Remember, too, that you'll have very good views perched up on bus seats, and that generally the buses are new and very comfortable. (Note that, outside Palma, you can flag down a bus anywhere along its route, without making for the centre of a village.)

The following two pages show you where to find your public transport in Palma; other public transport and taxi ranks are shown on various town plans in the text (see italicised type in index for town maps). On pages 159-161 you'll find the current public transport timetables, but *please do not rely solely on the timetables in this book*; changes to scheduling are fairly frequent. Obtain a listing from the Tourist Office in Palma (Avenida Rey Jaime III) as soon as you arrive! Finally, do remember that local transport will be much busier on Sundays and holidays.

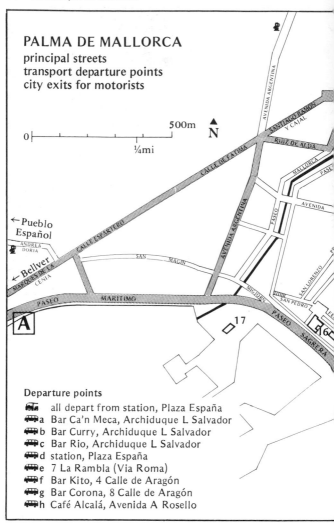

PALMA DE MALLORCA
principal streets
transport departure points
city exits for motorists

500m ▲ N

0 ├──────────────┤
        ¼mi

←Pueblo
Español

←Bellver

Departure points

🚌   all depart from station, Plaza España
🚌a Bar Ca'n Meca, Archiduque L Salvador
🚌b Bar Curry, Archiduque L Salvador
🚌c Bar Rio, Archiduque L Salvador
🚌d station, Plaza España
🚌e 7 La Rambla (Via Roma)
🚌f Bar Kito, 4 Calle de Aragón
🚌g Bar Corona, 8 Calle de Aragón
🚌h Café Alcalá, Avenida A Rosello

Where to find your transport in Palma

Destination	🚌	Destination	🚌	Destination	🚌
Alaró (also 🚆)	d	Campanet	f	Pollensa and Port	d
Alcudia and Port	d	Ca'n Picafort	d	Porto Cristo	d
Andraitx and Port	e	Colonia San Jordi	h	Porto Petro	h
Artá	d	Deiá	a	Puerto de Soller	a
Banyalbufar	c	Esporles	c	San Telmo	e
Bunyola (also 🚆)	b	Estellenchs	c	Santa Eugenia	g
Caimari	h	Felanitx	d	Santa María	🚆
Cala Bona	d	Inca (also 🚆)	h	Santanyí	h
Cala d'Or	h	Manacor	d	Selva	h
Cala Ratjada	d	Moscari	h	Ses Salines	h
Cala San Vicente	d	Paguera	e	Soller	🚆
Calas de Mallorca	d	Petra	d	Valldemossa	a

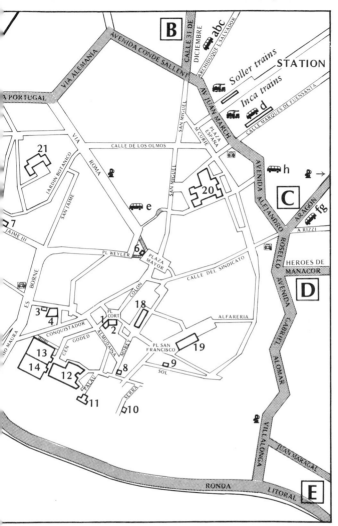

Key

- 🚌 bus departure points (a–h)
- 🚕 principal taxi ranks
- ⛽ principal petrol stations
1. museum (arts and crafts)
2. town hall
3. police station
4. post office
5. US consulate
6. British consulate
7. tourist information*
8. Oleza palace
9. Marques de Palmer palace
10. Arab baths
11. Episcopal palace (museum)
12. cathedral
13. military headquarters
14. Almudaina palace (museum)
15. La Lonja (fine arts museum)
16. maritime museum
17. Club Náutico
18. St Eulalia church
19. San Francisco church
20. market
21. hospital

also information kiosk in the Plaza España, opposite the station

Picnicking

Picnicking can be great fun on Mallorca, provided you choose either an established picnic site created by ICONA or an open area along the course of one of the walks. Much of Mallorca's land is in private hands — although it might *appear* to be open countryside. So **never** cross boundary fences, or picnic in enclosed fields, or you might find yourselves confronted by an irate landowner!

ICONA

These letters stand for El Instituto Nacional para la **Conservación de la Naturaleza**. Our National Institute for Nature Conservation has recently taken over several areas of the island, to convert them into beauty spots for public enjoyment. ICONA has also created several picnic areas, which were sadly lacking on the island — three of these being on the C710 between Lluc and Pollensa. They're very well equipped, with special brick ovens for roasting meat, wooden trestles and benches under the trees, outdoor water taps and modern WC facilities. Everything is spread out, so that you're not 'on top of' everyone else!

Other ICONA areas include the picnic site near the Playa de Coll Baix on the Aucanada peninsula (Walk 22) and the extensive area of the Cairats valley, near Valldemossa (Walk 5).

All *roadside* picnic areas *with tables* (and sometimes other facilities) are indicated both in the car tour notes and on the colour map by the symbol ⚊.

Picnic suggestions

If you prefer a 'get away from it all' picnic — or if you find that the established sites are too crowded (possible in the summer season and on Sundays and holidays), why not try a picnic spot along the course of one of the walks?

All the information you need to get to these 'private' picnics is given on the following pages, where *picnic numbers correspond to walk numbers*, so that you can quickly find the general location on the island by looking at the colour map. Under each picnic description, you'll find walking times, map reference and transport details (🚌, 🚂 means that the picnic is especially suitable for those using public transport — either bus or train; 🚗 indicates a picnic spot most suitable for those travelling by car). The exact location of the picnic spot is shown on the appropriate *walking map* by the symbol ℗, printed in red.

Please remember that these picnic suggestions are 'off the beaten track': you will want to wear sensible shoes and perhaps a **sunhat** (○ alerts you to a picnic spot in full sun). It's a good idea to take along a plastic sheet as well, in case the ground is damp.

To choose a spot that appeals to you, turn to the fold-out between pages 20 and 21. Here, on the reverse of the colour map, is a key to the photographs — one for each picnic.

If you're travelling to your picnic by public transport, refer to the timetables on pages 159—161. Here you may find more convenient scheduling than that given for the corresponding (long) walk. **If you are travelling in a hired car,** watch out for animals and children on the country roads, and always drive carefully through villages, where children often play in the streets. Without damaging plants, do park *well off* the road; **never** block a road or track!

All picnickers should read the country code on page 64 and go quietly in the countryside.

1 FROM SAN TELMO (map p71) 🚌 🚗
Choose shade or sun for this picnic, on a low headland overlooking the Isle of Dragonera. Only 15-20 minutes walking from the bus stop, or a couple of minutes on foot if you come by car.

Turn right at San Telmo, skirting the headland and following signs to 'Vista Dragonera'. Just before the tarmac road ends, turn up right on the earth track to park and picnic.

2 FROM ESPORLES (map p73) 🚗
Five to ten minutes walking from your car takes you to good picnicking in sun or shade, with countryside views.

Follow the road signed 'Es Verger' from the centre of Esporles, and use the notes on page 73 to start Walk 2.

3 FROM BUNYOLA (map p74) 🚆 🚌 🚗
Sunny or shaded picnicking overlooking olive-studded terraces, about 35 minutes' walk from the railway station. If you have a car, leave it at the Ca'n Penaso restaurant on the C710, saving a good 10 minutes.

Use the notes on page 74 to find the overlook, just past the second gate of the Alquería d'Avall farm.

4 FROM SANTA EUGENIA (map p77) 🚌 🚗 ○

About 20 minutes' easy climbing up from Santa Eugenia leads to a sunny picnic spot overlooking Es Pla (the plain). Can be windy in winter!

Your objective is the cross monument above the town; it's hard to believe, but from here almost the entire island is visible! This picnic walk starts from the Plaza España, the main square in Santa Eugenia, an uphill climb from the main road (PM304). You can leave your car here. Pass the bank and continue up the steep, winding tarmac road. Once onto a level tarmac track, turn right, and then left at the end, to go up a stony, walled-in track. Go through the gap in the wall at the top end of this track, to find the narrow, overgrown footpath up to the top of the hill. Climb the low stone wall and continue up to the cross monument.

5 FROM VALLDEMOSSA (map p80) 🚌 🚗

A picnic shaded by superb umbrella pines, overlooking Valldemossa. Under 20 minutes' walking from the village if you come by bus, or about 5 minutes if you travel by car.

If you're on foot, use the notes on page 78 to begin Walk 5; you'll reach the pines in under 20 minutes. If you're in a car, you can leave it in the new housing estate below the pines, but park neatly and do not obstruct any estate drives! The road into the estate is the first turning north off the Valldemossa—Palma road (PM111); from here follow the notes on page 78 to the start of the track to the pines.

6 FROM PUERTO DE SOLLER (map p82) 🚗

Picnic at the Torre Picada, overlooking the sea, or below the tower on a grassy slope.

Use the notes on page 82 to drive up the Carrer de Bélgica, out of Puerto de Soller, as far as the gates to the Torre Picada track. Leave your car by the gates, well tucked in. From here it's a walk of about 20 minutes to the tower, but there are good picnicking spots along the way as well. It can be windy at the cliff edge by the tower in winter, but there are sheltered, sunny — or shaded — spots below. *Take care if you picnic by the cliff edge, overlooking the sea!*

7 FROM SOLLER (map p84) 🚗

There's good picnicking not very far up the (steep) path of Es Barranc, on grassy terraces, populated by olive groves, overlooking the Soller valley.

The starting point is really Biniaraix, a short drive from Soller. Leave your car well tucked in, and use the notes for Walk 7 to follow a short way up the footpath signed 'Camí

Best reached by: 🚌 bus, 🚗 car, 🚂 train, ⛵ boat; ○ — in full sun d'es Barranc'. If you come by train, consider taking a taxi from Soller station to Biniaraix: you'll have only a short 10-15 minute climb up Es Barranc weighted down with your picnic, and you can stroll back downhill to Soller afterwards (about 45 minutes).

8 FROM MIRADOR DE SES BARQUES (map p94) 🚌* 🚗

A picnic in a wonderland of olive groves and stone terraces, a sheltered sun-trap in winter.

Leave your transport at the Mirador de Ses Barques and follow the notes for Walk 8 for as long as you like. There's good picnicking only 5 minutes into the walk, but if you go as far as the Font de Bálitx (20min), you'll find some welcome shade on a hot summer's day.

9a FROM LA CALOBRA (map p98) ⛴ 🚗 ○

You can picnic on the beach, in the sun (and in the company of day trippers), or you can venture up inside the gorge, where there are many good picnicking spots — but very little shade.

Leave your transport at La Calobra and explore inside the gorge as far as you like.

9b FROM ESCORCA (map p99) 🚌* 🚗

Picnic spots abound at Escorca — in full sun or shade.

Leave your transport at the Escorca restaurant on the C710 and use the notes for Walk 9 to start down the path behind the old church of Sant Pere. You'll find good picnicking in two minutes — or overlook the gorge in 15 minutes.

10 PUIG MAYOR (map p100) 🚗

Several superb picnic spots on the northern slopes of Mallorca's highest mountain — in sun or shade.

The starting point is the K2.2 marker on the La Calobra road, so this picnic is not easily accessible by public transport. Leave your car in the (small) parking area, making certain that you do not block the road! Follow the notes for Walk 10 as far as you like; there's good picnicking as soon as you finish the initial 15-minute climb. Perhaps the best spot is in the shade of the oaks (35min).

11 GORG BLAU (map p104) 🚌* 🚗

Not far into the course of Walk 11 — just an easy stroll from where you leave your car or bus — there's excellent picnicking way above the C710, overlooking the Gorge Blau. If you prefer a picnic just beside the water's edge, choose the Cuber reservoir, an area under the protection of ICONA.

Use notes p130; ten minutes walking gives good views, but after 30 minutes there's a splendid, shaded promontory.

🚌* see **STOP PRESS**, page 168, for bus details

12 PUIG DE MASSANELLA (FROM LLUC) (map p109) 🚌 ▣

A shady picnic spot at a 'sitja', under five minutes' walking from the gates to the Puig de Massanella.

Leave your transport at the petrol station on the PM213 south of Lluc. Walk downhill 150m (yds) to the Massanella gates on the right. Follow the track, forking up right before the farm building, to find the shady *sitja* on your right, by a rock outcropping. There are no far-reaching views, just mossy banks and the shade of oaks. For sun and views, you'll have to climb on for another 15-20 minutes.

13 LLUC VALLEY OVERLOOK (map p113) 🚌* ▣

A shady picnic under five minutes' walking from the monastery.

Leave your transport at Lluc and go to the monastery forecourt. A narrow tarmac lane leads northwest, between the bar-café left and the monastery right. In under five minutes you'll come to a rocky outcropping on the right, with shade and splendid views. Further down the valley are some of the oldest olive trees on Mallorca and fields steeped in wild flowers — but picnic near the roadside, not on farmland!

14 BINIFALDO ROAD (FROM LLUC) (map p115) 🚌* ▣

Sun or shade, and many good picnicking spots are to be found on the road to the Binifaldó spring-water bottling plant.

This picnic is especially suitable if you are travelling by car and find that the established ICONA sites are rather full, since there's ample parking space on the Binifaldó road — as long as you pull *well off* to the side, and watch out for the heavy lorries coming down from the bottling plant. Find the entrance to Binifaldó on the C710, just by the K17.4 marker (a sign here reads 'Ministerio de Agricultura. Jefatura Principal de ICONA ...'. If you travel by bus, you can either start from Lluc, by following the course of Walk 14 (about 30 minutes' walking), or use the bus along the C710 (see page 168) and ask for 'Binifaldó'.

15 FROM CAMPANET (map p123) ▣

A picnic by an old chapel, easily reached by car and very near to the Cuevas de Campanet. Not very convenient by bus — but an easy hour's walk from Campanet.

The charming Oratorio de San Miguel lies on the old Pollensa road, just south of the entrance to the Campanet caves, on the opposite side of the road. It is shown on most touring maps. If you approach it from Campanet, follow the (tortuous) village signposting for the caves, which take you to the old Pollensa road.

🚌* see **STOP PRESS**, page 168, for bus details

16 MORTITX (FROM POLLENSA) (map p128) 🚐* 🚗

Picnic in a 'wild-west' setting of wonderfully-formed rocks and gnarled trees — there's little shade.

The gates to Mortitx lie between the 10 and 11 Km markers on the C710, about 20 minutes' driving west of Pollensa. There's only room for one or two cars to park here; if you're not in luck, try one of the ICONA sites or Picnic 13 or 14. Follow the course of Walk 16 for as long as you like, but you'll find good picnic spots within 20 minutes at most.

17 TERNELLES (FROM POLLENSA) (maps pp130, 132) 🚐 🚗

The walk to this picnic is longer than any of the others — about one hour. But it's a very easy walk along a country lane, with so much to see along the way, that it's highly recommended.

Most current motoring maps show a motor road leading from Pollensa as far as the Castell del Rei. In fact, you cannot drive to Castell del Rei, but only as far as the gates to the Ternelles farm. But even driving to Ternelles is not recommended; the road is very narrow, with little room to turn the car round, and there is only room for one car to park by the Ternelles gates. Far better to start out on this picnic in Pollensa, using the notes for Walk 17. You can see the Roman bridge and have ample time to enjoy the lovely country road to Ternelles — without wondering if you're going to meet another car coming in the opposite direction. Picnic by the lovely stream, beyond the Ternelles gates.

18 FROM POLLENSA (maps pp130, 134) 🚐 🚗

A shady or sunny picnic, overlooking Pollensa or Alcudia's bay.

By car you can drive part way up the Puig de María (the lane lies on the south side of the PM220, by the K51.9 marker). Leave your car where the road ends, and follow the course of Walk 18 for under 10 minutes for splendid views of Pollensa, or for 20 minutes to overlook Alcudia. If you come by bus from Palma, ask to be put off at 'Puig de María', and add about five minutes to the above times. If you come by bus from Soller (see page 168), use the map on page 130 to find the lane to the Puig de María.

19 FROM CALA SAN VICENTE (map p136) 🚐 🚗 ○

A picnic in full sun, overlooking the Formentor headlands.

The starting point is the Hotel Don Pedro in Cala San Vicente. From there, use the notes for Short walk 19 to find your picnic spot in about 10—20 minutes easy climbing — there are many fine overlooks from 'Eagle Mountain'.

Best reached by: 🚐 bus, 🚗 car; ○ — in full sun

20 FROM PUERTO DE POLLENSA (map p137) 🚌 📷

A picnic under pines, overlooking the Boquer valley, a setting of special interest to bird-watchers — so take binoculars along!

By bus use notes for Short Walk 20 — a 35-minute walk. By car, park at the Boquer gates, saving 15 minutes.

21 FROM PUERTO DE POLLENSA (map p137) 📷 ○

A short walk on the track to the Albercutx watchtower affords splendid views of the Formentor headlands, but no shade at all.

Leave your car at the Mirador d'es Colomer and follow the start of Walk 21 until you find a setting that pleases.

22 FROM ALCUDIA (maps pp140, 141) 📷

Two picnicking possibilities on the Aucanada peninsula, both with ample shade. If you want to go by taxi from Alcudia, see the hints on page 158, to ask the driver to take you to one of the picnic spots and return for you in time for the last bus.

The first picnic overlooks Pollensa's bay and is reached from the Ermita de la Victoria (see car touring notes, p35). Park here and follow Short walk 22 up towards Peña Roja for at least ten minutes for good views — the best views are reached after 20 minutes' climbing. The second choice is Mount Victoria Park: follow car tour notes on page 35, but turn right just in front of the Bodega del Sol bar. Leave your car inside the park gates and picnic anywhere; the outlook over Aucanada's lighthouse is 1.4km past the gates.

23 BETLEM (FROM ARTA) (map p143) 📷

Superb views of both the coast and the Artá range.

Use the car touring notes on page 39 to find Betlem, east of the Colonia de San Pedro. Then follow the indications in the notes and on the map for Walk 23 to enjoy this picnic, walking only for as long as you like.

24 FROM ARTA (map p145) 📷

A shady picnic overlooking a lovely, sandy cove — about 15 minutes' walking from where you leave your car.

Use the notes in *italic type* on page 145 to find the road out of Artá that leads to Cala Estreta (this road is not on most motoring maps). Park here and then follow the notes for Walk 24 to picnic in the trees just beyond Cala Matzocs.

25 FROM CALA RATJADA (map p148) 🚌 📷

You can find sun or shade at the lovely beach of Cala Guya, but in summer you're likely to find an overspill of tourists from Cala Ratjada keeping you company — so best to make this an 'out of season' picnic choice.

Use the notes for Walk 25 to drive or walk from Cala Ratjada to Cala Guya, where you can picnic on the beach or on the rocky finger of 'Es Guyó'.

Touring

The ideal way to tour Mallorca is by car, of course. Most of the island's roads are in very good condition; many have been re-surfaced in recent years in an attempt to improve driving conditions. The mountainous west coast is the most popular side of the island, with spectacular scenery that you must not miss. The east coast has its own distinct flavour, and touring here is especially enjoyable in spring or summer months when you can take advantage of the idyllic beaches.

Car hire

Remember that it's wise to shop around, because car hire prices vary quite a bit. As a generalisation, prices at the local firms are lower than those of international chains.

Be sure that you understand the terms of the hire agreement that you have signed and what the insurance covers. You will need a current driving licence, and *only* those people whose licence numbers and names have been written on the agreement will be covered by insurance to drive the car. *Do* check the car carefully for damage before you take it on the road. You will also be expected to pay a (cash) deposit against insurance and a full take of petrol when you sign the agreement; you will be refunded to the value of any petrol in the car when you return it. (And note that many petrol stations are closed Sundays and holidays!)

Motoring laws

All road signs on Mallorca are international, except for the 'give way' sign, which reads *ceda el paso*. The following laws are strictly enforced:

- **Right of way** must be given to any vehicle coming from your *right*, unless otherwise indicated.
- Front-seat passengers must wear **seat belts**, and children are not permitted in the front seats until they are old enough to wear seat belts.
- **Unbroken lines** in the centre of the road must not be crossed.
- **Three-point turns** and **reversing into side streets** are forbidden in built-up areas.
- **Parking** facing oncoming traffic is prohibited; also parking on any very narrow or one-way roads.

Speed limits vary, at the time of writing: 130km per hour on motorways; 110km per hour on the 'C' roads, 90km per hour on other roads, and 40km per hour (unless otherwise indicated) in towns and villages. But when planning your tour, remember that you won't cover more than about 35km an hour on the winding mountain roads. Always **allow for delays** along some of the main and mountain roads during the summer season, and especially on Sundays, when all the 'week-enders' are returning to Palma. And **allow plenty of time for stops**: the driving times given only include short breaks at the viewpoints labelled (☜) in the text.

Most of the larger villages have **repairs garages**; these are often next to the petrol station. There are **telephone booths** in nearly all villages, usually found in the main square. **Toilet facilities** are found at bar-cafés and restaurants and most petrol stations; other public toilets are indicated in the notes by WC. Apart from the emergency medical centres shown in the notes (⊕), many beaches have **first-aid kiosks** *in summer*.

The touring notes

Recognising that most people stay around Palma, the ten excursions described all fan out from the capital, covering the island in clockwise fashion. The notes themselves are very brief: they include little material that you can obtain free from the various tourist information kiosks. Instead, I've concentrated on the 'logistics' of touring: times and distances, road conditions, facilities en route, etc.

Most of all, these touring notes emphasise possibilities for **walking** (if you team up with walkers, you may lower your car hire costs) and **picnicking**. While some of the picnic suggestions may not be convenient during a long car tour, you may see a landscape that you would like to explore at leisure another day.

The fold-out colour map is designed to be held out opposite the touring notes and contains all the information you should need outside Palma; the city exits key in with those on the Palma map on pages 10–11.

Various symbols have been used in the text and on the colour map, to show you the location of different facilities or points of interest *at a glance*:

km	*cumulative* km *from Palma*	✗	restaurant
⬧	petrol, car servicing	▲/♠	hotel/inn, hostelry
♦/♣	monastery/church, chapel	★	tourist attraction
⊕	emergency medical centre	M	museum
✗	picnic site with tables	℗	picnic reference with
☜	viewpoint *with parking*		number (see pp12-18)

1 SPECTACULAR SOUTHWEST SETTINGS

Paguera · Puerto de Andraitx · Andraitx · San Telmo ·
Estellenchs · Banyalbufar · La Granja · Esporles · Palma

104km/65mi; about 5 hours driving; Exit A from Palma (map p10)

On route: no **X**; Ⓟ1, 2; Walks 1, 2

*A leisurely all-day tour – or perhaps one for a long summer
afternoon. The roads are generally in good condition, but are
often narrow and winding. La Granja is open daily (except
Sundays) from April to October; open Wednesdays and
Thursdays the rest of the year. Tickets may be purchased at
the entrance; hours 15.30–17.30 only*

Leave Palma by driving west on the beautiful, palm-
shaded Paseo Marítimo (Exit A), passing beside the
commercial port and naval zone of **Porto Pí**. Continue
straight ahead on to the new motorway, in the direction
of Andraitx. Along here you will have excellent views of
the various coastal tourist resorts, without having to drive
laboriously through them! The motorway climbs gradually, above the popular resort of Cala Mayor, where a
series of small beaches and elegant hotels attracts many
sun-seekers. Soon the Castillo de Bendinat appears on the
left (8km) – a beautiful neo-Gothic palace surrounded
by parklands. Continuing along the *autopista* we pass by
the tourist areas of Illetas, Portals Nous, and Palma Nova;
then the motorway ends at the C719 (🏠 at 18km).

Not much further along we come to **Paguera** (23km
🏨 ✕⊕), another splendid coastal resort boasting three
beaches — their sand dunes shaded by pines. Drive carefully through the main thoroughfare, between bar-cafés
with brightly-coloured awnings and souvenir shops. We
leave the main road at **Camp de Mar**, turning left uphill
on the pretty PM101/2 and winding along into scenic
Puerto de Andraitx (31km 🏨✕🏠), where a conglomeration of expensive yachts, fishing boats and all kinds of
sea-craft bob gently up and down together. After a brief
visit and refreshment at a port-side café, it's worth while
to walk – or drive – along the headland of Sa Mola,
from where you can enjoy the coastal views and the
outlook to the nearby Isle of Sa Dragonera, which we'll
see from a different perspective later in the tour.

Leaving the picturesque harbour behind you, climb
the C719 towards the town, famous for its almond
orchards and breathtakingly beautiful early on in the
year, when a 'snowfall' of delicate blossom covers the
valley. Enter **Andraitx** (36km 🏠🏨✕🏠), where a colourful
open-air market fills the streets on Wednesdays. At the

21

junction, turn left towards Estellenchs (signposted). Then, some 400 metres further on, the C710 branches off to the right, just by a second signpost to Estellenchs.

But before continuing along this main coastal road, we turn left again almost at once, on the PM103, another meandering country road leading to the peaceful and attractive resort of **San Telmo** (44km 🏨 ✕). Walk 1, which visits an ancient Trappist monastery, begins here in the island's westernmost village. If you'd like to stretch your legs, why not try one of the short versions of this walk? You'll be passing the starting point when, after arriving in San Telmo, you turn right and continue along the coastal road until it comes to an end at 'Vista Dragonera', from where you have superb views of that island (and excellent picnicking just on the headland to your right — see Ⓟ1). Before returning to the C710, you may wish to pass by the Castle of San Telmo on the south side of the village, but it is unfortunately not open to the public.

Rejoining the C710 (53km), we wind up through a green landscape of pine-clad hills and mountains towards the rugged, western coastline of steep cliffs and rocky inlets — mostly inaccessible except by sea. As we climb higher, the beauty of Andraitx and its harbour can really be appreciated. Do not attempt more than about 30km per hour along this winding mountain road, frequented by tourist coaches. We begin to catch glimpses of the sea again now, and soon we can stop off at the Mirador de Ses Ortigues (63km 📷). Climb up the fallen rocks to the right for a good view of the rocky cove of La Cala de Ses Ortigues below. The coastal road continues now, affording excellent vistas all along, passing by a second viewpoint (65km 📷). Then a few more minutes brings us to the attractive cliff-top restaurant of Es Grau (67km ✕) and the adjoining **Mirador R Roca★** (📷). Take the stone steps at the right of the parking area up to the *mirador*, for some really splendid views of this wild and rocky stretch of coast. Then you might like to try some fresh grilled prawns (very reasonably priced) on the open-air terrace of the restaurant, overlooking the sea. A tourist shop here sells hand-made articles, such as lace and woven baskets, as well as the usual souvenirs.

The C710 now dives down through the tunnel of Es Grau and hugs the coast. At the Coll d'es Pí (71km ✕🍷📷), the road turns inland and down into **Estellenchs** (72km 🛉🏨✕). The village sits at the foot of Mount Galatzó, where orange groves and olive trees populate the fertile terraced slopes, irrigated by mountain springs. The road narrows as it leaves

the village and snakes its way to the **Talaia de Ses Animes**★ (78km 📷). Cross the narrow bridge to climb up inside the old watchtower (*talaia* in the Mallorcan dialect) for more magnificent views of the coast.

Further along, we come into **Banyalbufar** (81km 🏨✕), set on slopes above the sea. The secret of these well-kept, fertile terraces is the irrigation system. Waters from mountain springs are channelled along through stone *canaletas* (water courses) to irrigate the entire area (see also page 154).

The road now swings inland once more, as it winds through thick pine forests. Some sharp bends will require maximum concentration and minimum speed. Just before the junction of the PM110, you'll find space to stop the car for a fabulous view of the mountains to the northeast around Valldemossa. Then fork right towards Esporles.

We pass a road off right to Puigpunyent and then find the signposted entrance to **La Granja**★ (89km). This large and splendid house once belonged to Cistercian monks, and later to an aristocratic Mallorcan family, but the archways and ornamental fountains evoke its Moorish past. Women in traditional Mallorcan costume invite you to taste delicious home-made *buñuelos* and other typical Mallorcan cakes, sample the wines, and visit the house, museum and grounds for a modest entrance fee. From Tuesdays to Fridays, at extra cost, a lively exhibition of folk dancing makes this a really worthwhile visit.

On the homeward route now, a lovely avenue of planes welcomes us into **Esporles** (92km 🛈), a curious village built along both sides of a stream. You might like to stop here and visit the thirteenth-century church. Here, also, the road in the centre of the village, signed to 'Es Verger' is the starting point for Walk 2, which visits the pretty Ermita de Maristela, and for a quiet countryside picnic (℗2).

Past Esporles, meet a junction at 93km and take the right-hand PM104, coming to **Establiments** (99km), where Chopin and George Sand first lived before taking up residence at Valldemossa. The final stretch of the tour (🍴 at 101km) brings us into the centre of Palma at the joining of the Via Alemania and the Avenida Conde Sallent (104km).

2 PRETTY MOUNTAIN VILLAGES

Valldemossa · Puerto de Valldemossa · La Ermita de la
Trinidad · El Mirador de Ses Pitas · Son Marroig · Deiá ·
Lluc-Alcari · Puerto de Soller · Gardens of Alfabia · Palma
86km/53mi; about 4 hours driving; Exit B from Palma (map p11)
On route: no X; Ⓟ 3, 5, 6; Walks 3, 5, 6,
*This drive takes only a few hours, but I suggest you make a full
day of it — there are so many interesting things to see and places to
visit along the way! Entrance tickets are available at the gates for:*
*The Carthusian Monastery (Valldemossa): open daily except Sundays
from 09.30—13.00 and from 15.00—18.30 (17.30 in winter); closed
some holidays*
Son Marroig (Deiá): open daily 09.00—12.00 and 15.00—20.00
*Alfabia Gardens: open daily except Sundays from 09.30—13.00 and
15.00—18.00 (17.00 in winter); closed some holidays*

From the Avenida Conde de Sallent, take the Calle 31 de
Diciembre (Exit B — the beginning of the C711 to Soller
and signposted). On the outskirts of town, passing by the
Red Cross clinic on the right, follow the signs that read
'Valldemossa', out onto the country road, the PM111 (🛢 at
9km). At the junction (10km) keep right, following the sign
to Valldemossa, through almond orchards and farmlands,
towards the lower, pine-covered foothills below the *sierra*.
The glass-blowing factory on the left, at Esglaieta (11km),
makes a brief, but interesting stop-off. Now the road starts
to climb gradually, through vast olive orchards and pines,
towards the picturesque mountain village where Chopin and
George Sand lived during the winter of 1838-9. The blue-
topped bell-tower of the monastery where they rented cells
is clearly visible from the road as it winds its way on up
between the low hills.

Enter Valldemossa★ (17km ♠♠♠X℗5): turn left, and
then right, and you can park in front of the monastery.
Originally the site of a Moorish palace, the buildings were
later the retreat of King Sancho. After his death, the place
was given to Carthusian monks who, little by little, constructed the monastery. When this religious order was
expelled from Spain in 1835, private owners took over and
rented the cells to travellers (the famous Spanish poet,
Ruben Dario, also lived here for a short while at the beginning of this century). Join the throngs to visit Chopin's
quarters, which contain his piano, death mask and some
original manuscripts. The old pharmacy is fascinating. The
church, of neo-classical type, is especially interesting because
of the frescoes painted in the vaults by Miguel Bayeu,
brother-in-law to Goya. At King Sancho's palace, you can
see exhibitions of Mallorcan folk-dancing at 11.00 on

Wednesdays and Thursdays. A nearby tourist shop sells hand-embroidered shawls and carved olive-wood objects.

Leave the village along the main road, in the direction of Andraitx—Soller (signposted). At 19km, the C710 branches off right towards Deiá. But we'll continue ahead for another few hundred metres, and find a narrow turning off right. Drive *very carefully* down this narrow, tortuous road, which twists its way down the mountainside towards the sea, where the hamlet of **Puerto de Valldemossa** (23km ✕) shelters amongst the rocks. Quaint little fishermen's dwellings crowd around the tiny marina and straddle up the rocky hillside. Recently the beginnings of a tourist urbanisation have begun to take root here. At the bar-restaurant overlooking the quay, a very typical dish, *arroz de pescado* (fish and rice soup), warms the stomach on a chilly day.

Return to the coastal C710 now, and turn left towards Deiá (♣ at 28km). But just about another kilometre further along, keep a sharp lookout for the narrow turning up right to the **Ermita de la Trinidad** (29km ♦♦☞). The way is so narrow that only one car can get through — so hope that you don't meet anybody coming in the opposite direction! However, once at the top, there is plenty of room for parking and turning. Visit the tiny chapel and small interior patios, from where you can enjoy a truly marvellous view of the coastline below.

Again rejoining the C710, sitting on the clifftops almost opposite the turning up to the *ermita* is the **Mirador de Ses Pitas** (30km ✕☞). From this viewpoint, you can see the old house at S'Estaca, where the Archduke Luis Salvador spent many hours with his young lover, Catalina Homar. Continuing along the coastal road (✕ at 32km) and passing through Miramar (an early acquisition of Luis Salvador), we begin to catch glimpses of La Foradada (the rock pierced with a hole), a rocky promontory jutting out into the sea.

It's not long before we come to **Son Marroig★** (34km ✕☞M), the elegant principal residence of the Archduke Luis Salvador of Austria. Two superb viewpoints permit excellent photos of La Foradada below. Visit the Italian marble *mirador*, specially made for him and transported here — a poetic reminder of a romantic past, where silent memories haunt the gardens. Then go into the house: a guided tour of the rooms containing the original furniture, plus several of his excellent sketches and paintings, photos and portraits of his family, amply repays the small cost of the entrance fee. Luis Salvador's exceptional love for Mallorca's natural history (see also page 79) is very much in evidence.

Our route continues along the coast, passing by another viewpoint (☞) at 35km, and soon comes into the pretty mountain village of **Deiá** (37km ♦♠✕M), home of many well-known artists and poets — Robert Graves being one of the earliest to settle here. A stop-off can include a visit to the small but extremely interesting archaeological museum and the church on the hill above the village, which has a charming cemetery. A small road leads down to a pebble beach at the Cala de Deiá. The C710 twists its way through the village (you might be tempted to stop at the shop just past the centre, where hand-made goods and *artesanía* are sold), and then weaves its way between mountains and rocky coast towards Soller. On the way we pass through another artist's colony you might like to visit — the small hamlet of **Lluc-Alcari** (40km ♠).

Continuing on towards Soller (✕ at 43km), more splendid views unfold: the distant high peaks and lower mountains, pine-clad hillsides dotted with chalets, and later, the marvellous panorama of citrus and olive groves forming the basin of Soller below in the valley. As you approach the village, turn left onto the C711 and head for **Puerto de Soller** (50km ♠✕). Here, amidst sun-seekers, bright bar-cafés and crowded beaches, the summer comes into its own. On the other hand, a rather desolate scene denotes the winter season. At any time of year, however, a short walk uphill to the Torre Picada (Ⓟ6), will be rewarded by a wonderfully scenic vista of the port and its surrounding coastline.

Return along the C711 back past Soller village (♣ at 55km). Now the road begins to snake in interminable bends up towards the mountain pass, the Coll de Soller. More superb views of the setting can be had from the *mirador* just below the pass (62km ☞). On the south side of the *coll*, we soon come to another viewpoint by a mountaintop restaurant (63km ✕☞), this time overlooking Palma bay.

Winding on down the mountain, through endless olive slopes, it is not long before we can again stretch our legs at the **Gardens of Alfabia★** (69km WC✕), while we explore the exotic pavilions, romantic arbours, and bamboo-shaded lily ponds. Our homeward stretch (✕ and Ⓟ3 at 71km, ♣ at 84km) brings us into Palma's *avenidas* at Exit B (86km).

3 THE MAGNIFICENT MOUNTAIN ROUTE

Soller · Biniaraix · Fornalutx · Mirador de Ses Barques ·
Gorg Blau · La Calobra · Caimari · Selva · Inca · Palma
136km/85mi; about 6 hours driving; Exit B from Palma (map p11)
On route: ✗ at the Mirador de Ses Barques and the PM213 between
Lluc and Caimari; ℗3, 7-12; Walks 3, 7-12

*This beautiful drive passes through some of the most spectacular
mountain scenery on the island, and it is generally the most popular
route. Therefore, although the roads are in good condition, heavy
traffic will slow you down considerably, especially in summer.
Expect to meet coaches. Many hairpin bends throughout, but
especially on the tortuous narrow road to La Calobra, make this a
route for the experienced driver only. Of all our tours, this is the
one you must not miss — so do consider a coach tour, if you want a
more relaxing day*

Leaving Palma from the *avenidas*, we take the C711 out
of the city (Exit B), in the direction of Soller (♟ at 2.5
and 3km). You'll see the grand old country mansion of Son
Amar, now sadly converted into a tourist barbeque spot.
On a bright morning early in the year, this road is at its
best. It heads straight as an arrow across the plain through
dazzlingly bright pink and white almond orchards towards
the sombre mountain range beyond, where the sun has not
yet lighted the *sierra*. We pass by ✗ and ℗3 at 15km and
the **Gardens of Alfabia★** (Tour 2) at 17km. Then the road
starts to climb in earnest, winding up to the south side of
the Coll de Soller (23km ✗▦), with splendid overviews of
the plain and Palma's bay. Then, just over the pass, we find
a second *mirador* (▦), from where the panoramic view of
Soller in the valley, entirely surrounded by high mountains,
is breathtakingly beautiful. Go *carefully* now, round countless hairpin bends, watching out for tourist-loaded coaches
on the tight corners. Follow the road as it winds down into
the valley, over the small bridge,
and towards the sea. At the first
opportunity, we leave the C711
at a signposted turning right into
Soller★ (33km ✝▲✗). The village
is a popular tourist destination
not only because of the beauty
of its setting, but it's also such
fun to get about here, on the
charming narrow-gauge railway
and the tram to Puerto de Soller.

Drive slowly down the narrow streets (you may find the
sketch-map of Soller on page 88 helpful), to come to the
Plaça de Sa Constitució (Constitution Square). Before us is
the 16th-century church, with its lovely neo-Gothic façade.

Continue on round the square and you'll soon see the signpost to Biniaraix — pointing us to the right, down a narrow but animated street, full of busy shoppers, where the tangy scents range from carved olive-wood to freshly-baked bread. Driving — again, very slowly — along this narrow road, we continue on to **Biniaraix** (35km ♦ and ℗7). Many mountain footpaths radiate from this quaint little village nestling in the mountains amongst orange groves; one of the best is the old pilgrims' trail up Es Barranc (see Walk 7). In the hamlet, turn right into the Calle San José, a very narrow street. At the end, we turn left down an equally narrow lane that leaves Biniaraix behind and winds on between beautiful chalets and orange orchards. There are some excellent views of Soller from here.

Coming now to a wider road, we turn right, passing by the stream, and come into **Fornalutx** (37km ♦ ✗), which must surely be the most picturesque village on Mallorca. You can park in the small leafy square and explore up the stone steps, along quaint cobbled streets, where open doorways show beautiful Mallorcan interiors. And you'll probably want to visit the old church.

From the square at Fornalutx, take the continuing road to the right, which now climbs up above the village, through a scenic landscape of orange groves and olive orchards on terraced slopes. Here, also, there are some wonderful vistas of the Soller valley. Eventually we come to the road junction, where we turn right on the C710, in the direction of Lluc and Pollensa (signposted). This mountain road climbs to amazing heights, affording breathtaking views of the valley and coastline, before we come to the fabulous **Mirador de Ses Barques★** (40km ✗⌨✗℗8), famous for its freshly squeezed orange juice. The view from the top terrace is simply spectacular: we can see the wide arc of the bay of Soller, its port and lighthouse, the Torre Picada (Walk 6) on the headland, the rugged circle of mountains all round, and the deep aquamarine sea — all in one eagle's-eye panorama. Before you leave the *mirador*, be sure to use the notes on page 93 to make a five-minute walk towards Bálitx (℗8), where you'll see some of the island's most impressive stone-walled olive terracing.

Leaving the Mirador de Ses Barques, continue along the ever-climbing C710, passing more olive-terraced slopes and pines, heading towards the peaks. We can see the enormous Puig Mayor (1445m/4740ft) looming up ahead, and the air is decidedly fresher. After climbing steadily for a while, we come to a short tunnel (41km). Then, after passing a deep, terraced valley down below on the right, we meet the first long tunnel under the mountain (switch on your car lights), at the Coll d'es Puig Mayor (48km 📷).

Say 'goodbye' now to this scenery, or take your last snapshot from the viewpoint, for you will find that the landscape is completely different on the other side. Once your eyes have accustomed themselves to the daylight again, a tranquil, uninhabited panorama of green valleys and rocky mountains unfolds itself before you, as the road winds down to the Cuber valley, passing through the military zone of Son Torrellas. (Do not attempt to take photographs while driving through this area — your film might be confiscated.)

Soon we come to the Embalse de Cuber (📷), the Cuber reservoir, where there's good picnicking at the water's edge, and good trout fishing — if you obtain a licence in advance from ICONA. Just past the Cuber, we cross the modern aqueduct (Ⓟ11), and we round the south side of the Puig Mayor over to our left. Then we arrive at the second — larger — reservoir, the **Gorg Blau**, built in 1971 (54km 📷). Across the water, the keen eye can find some prehistoric columns, part of an ancient temple dating from the fifth century BC to the second century AD.

We now go through our second tunnel (55km) and leave the valley. It's not long before we reach the turn-off to La Calobra (PM214-1) at 56km, just by a bar-kiosk and small souvenir shop. The narrow, but fairly well-surfaced road climbs over the bare, rocky mountain (Ⓟ10 at K2.2 stone) and then finds its way down to the sea. It's a sinuous route, over a rugged landscape of mountains, rocks and pinnacles, giving fantastic views of the coast below, but is not for the inexperienced driver or those who may suffer from vertigo.

Many sharp bends later, we arrive at **La Calobra** (68km 🏨✕), a beautiful creek. Here, some of the most stunning and grandiose island scenery can be contemplated, at the **Torrente de Pareis★** (the twin streams), where a torrent flows between vertical rock cliffs almost 200m (535ft) high, towards the sea. A small shingle beach (Ⓟ9a) can be reached through an exciting tunnel under the rock. Boat trips run daily throughout the summer (see schedules page 161), and, if the sea is calm, this is decidedly the best way to view this wonderful part of the Mallorcan coast.

Return now to the C710 and pass under a lovely russet-stone Romanesque bridge spanning the road (81km). Turn left in the direction of Lluc (signposted), following the mountain route. Soon we can stop for a few minutes at the tiny Mirador de Escorca (84km 📷), where, looking over the

precipice, we can really appreciate the tremendous height of the gorge. Across the valley, the large old *carabineros* house (Walk 13) can be seen, abandoned on the hillside. Just beyond the *mirador* we find the chapel of Sant Pere (85km ♦✕), on the left, just opposite Escorca's restaurant. You may ask for the key at the restaurant: this is one of the oldest historical monuments on Mallorca. It's from this churchyard that the path (℗9a) leads down into the gorge, from where expert walkers can follow the course of the Pareis torrent — in summer months — as far as La Calobra (Walk 9).

From Escorca we continue as far as the next road junction (90km), where we meet the turning left to Lluc. Today we continue straight ahead however, in the direction of Inca (signposted) on the PM213 (♣ left), passing by the gates to the Puig de Massanella on our right (℗12). We gradually wind on down through the mountains, between pine- and oak-covered hills and valleys (◙ right at first set of S-bends, followed by ✕ on the left). Pass more fine olive-terracing and then come into the pretty village of **Caimari** (100km ♦), at the foot of the *sierra*. There's a lovely, easy walk from here to Binibona — see Short walk E, page 121.

Leaving the village we come upon undulating countryside, almond- and olive-covered foothills, and arrive shortly after at **Selva** (102km ♦), set on a hill and dominated by the square-towered church. If you make a stop here (perhaps to visit the weekly folklore festivals held on Tuesdays and Fridays throughout the year), be sure to visit the market, its entrance flanked by a beautiful avenue of cypresses.

Our next centre is **Inca** (106km ♠♦✕♣⊕), famous for its leather factories and wine cellars. Shoemakers have congregated in Inca since the eighteenth century, and a good export trade exists today. You may be interested in buying some leather goods at 'factory prices'. Most of the wine cellars have been converted into restaurants, and offer excellent meals in *típico* surroundings.

The one-way traffic system through Inca demands slow driving and a keen eye for the signposts to Palma! We meet the C713 and turn right for the last lap of the tour (the route is described, in reverse, on the facing page). A straight and easy run brings us into the city's *avenidas* on the Calle Aragón (Exit C), after an exhilarating 136km drive.

4 THE SIERRA AND THE CAPES

Santa María · Inca · Lluc · Pollensa · Puerto de Pollensa ·
Cabo de Formentor · Alcudia · Puerto de Alcudia · Mal Pas
(Cabo del Pinar) · Cuevas de Campanet · Palma

203km/126mi; about 7-8 hours driving; Exit C from Palma (map p11)

On route: ✗ on the PM213 between Caimari and Lluc; two ICONA
picnic areas on C710 between Lluc and Pollensa; S'Illot (Mal Pas);
at Ermita de la Victoria; ℗12-22; Walks 12-22

*Take a couple of days over this tour, if you can. If you make it a
one-day tour, do start out early in the morning. The beauty of the
capes is certainly worth the long drive from Palma (on excellent
roads), and a visit to the dream-like caves at Campanet (open daily
from 10.30–18.45) adds a perfect final touch to the excursion.*

From the *avenidas*, take the Calle Aragón (the road to
Inca — Exit C from Palma; ⚫ at 2km). This becomes the
C713 and passes the suburb of Pont d'Inca at about 4km.
The road continues straight ahead, out into the country,
and across the flat lands of the plain (⚫ at 7km; ✗ at 8km).
   The first village met is **Santa María** (14km ✗⚫⊕♦ and M
of natural history). The blue-belfried church is worth a visit,
as are the wine cellars and the leather goods factory (this
latter has an entrance marked by the trunk of a centuries-
old olive tree). Continuing along the C713, we pass through
Consell (17.5km ✗⊕) and a glassblowing factory on the left
just outside the village. **Binissalem** (22km ♦✗ and olive-
wood factory) is famous for its wines. Its church, which
dates back to the fourteenth century, is an interesting blend
of Gothic and Baroque architecture. Not much further along
is the **Foro de Mallorca★** (25km ✗M), a castle-like structure
housing a wax museum. Perhaps you've time at least for an
early-morning coffee by the pool.
   We soon reach **Inca** (28km ♦▲ ✗⚫⊕). Several leather
factories here sell their goods at amazingly low prices
(compared with Palma), but you would need a complete
morning just to browse, so today press on! Do not turn left
into Inca, but keep on towards Puerto de Alcudia as far as
the third set of traffic lights; here turn right, following signs
to Llubi; then *immediately* turn up left at the tiny roundabout for Lluc (the route is well signposted through Inca).
   Once out into the country again (⚫ at 31km), you'll
find the PM213 starts to climb steadily up into the foothills
towards the *sierra*, passing through **Selva** (34km, Tour 3),
and later winding on through fields of almond and olive
trees to **Caimari** (36km ♦), a picturesque village sheltering
at the foot of the mountains. Here our climb up to Lluc
begins, through thickly pine- and oak-wooded hills and
mountains. We pass by the first, shady picnic area (✗) at

39km. As we climb higher, we come to the famous 'Salto de la Bella Donna' at 42km (). This is not a fully-fledged *mirador*, but there's just room to leave your car on the gravel over at the left-hand side of the road. Legend has it that a pilgrim pushed his wife over the precipice here, while they were making a pilgrimage to Lluc on foot. When he later arrived at the sanctuary, he discovered his wife praying tranquilly before the image of the Virgin. The panorama from the 'Salto' is exceedingly wild and beautiful.

Continuing up to Lluc, we pass the gates to the Puig de Massanella (℗12) on the left and continue along (⚑✕ at 44km) until we meet a junction. Turn right here onto the C710 (✕ at 45km). Meet a second junction and fork up left, just past the camping site (WC), into **Lluc** (46.5km ⚫M✕⚑✕). You can leave your car in the large, free car park and, while the children romp about in the swing park, enjoy a thirst-quencher at the round bar-restaurant under the eucalyptus trees.

The monastery of Lluc is steeped in history and legend, originating during the eighth century, when a young shepherd was reported to have seen visions and strange lights in the sky, whereupon he discovered a carved image of the Virgin. Years later, this was deposited in the church of Sant Pere at Escorca (see page 30 and Walk 9), only to disappear and re-appear once again at Lluc — where a small chapel was then built. The present monastery building dates from the seventeenth and eighteenth centuries; the church itself, built between 1622 and 1724, was considerably altered at the beginning of the 1900s. Visitors come from all over the island to this important Catholic centre, and pilgrimages are often made on foot up to the sanctuary. An interesting museum contains coin collections, typical dress, and items of archaeological merit. Of most importance to lovers of Mallorca's countryside is the opportunity to stay overnight at the monastery — for this is the very best spot on the island from which to start on several superb walks!

Return from Lluc back to the T-junction, and take the C710 in the direction of Pollensa (signposted). Soon we pass two very complete ICONA picnic sites (⚔ WC) with tables, fireplaces, running water and toilet facilities. The first is on our left, and the second is on both sides of the road. The second one has a swing park for children, and, if you choose the site on the right-hand side of the road, there's an easy track leading off into the woods, with wonderful views of the Puig Tomir. For those who prefer a more secluded picnic, there are four possibilities between here and Pollensa (see Ⓟ13, 14, 16 and 17). If you've come out of season, you're likely to be able to park easily at any one of these spots; but in summer — or on holidays — your best best is Picnic 14. There's ample parking space on the Binifaldó road, and the picnicking is superb: there's sun or the shade of oaks, weirdly-formed rock 'tables', and splendid views.

The narrow road snakes its way through more strange rock formations, through a dramatic — almost savage — landscape of bare mountains, sparsely populated by ancient olive trees. Gradually, the picturesque route finds its way down towards the northern end of the island, where a magnificent vista of the Bay of Pollensa is seen from the road.

Continuing on down (✗ at 64km), it is not long before we come into **Pollensa** (66km ♂♂ ✗🍷), a market garden town some six kilometres from the coast. Just by the side of the C710, near the entrance to the town and almost opposite the signpost to Ternelles (Ⓟ17), a Roman bridge★ — the only one of its kind on Mallorca — still stands over the Torrente de San Jordi.

If you decide to enter Pollensa, make a point of visiting the cypress-bordered stone stairway that leads up the Calvary Hill★ to a tiny eighteenth-century chapel, from where there is a glorious view of the bays of Pollensa and Alcudia. There are 365 steps, one for each day of the year. From here you can also see the Puig de Maria (Ⓟ18), almost opposite, on the other side of the town. Rising to 333m (1090ft), this peak also commands fine views of the bays, valleys and mountains around Pollensa.

Leaving Pollensa, continue straight ahead (the route is now numbered PM220), to make for the port. You'll pass the side road off to Cala San Vicente (Ⓟ19) on the left at 68km, and then come to **Puerto de Pollensa** (72km 🏨 ✕🏰⊕M) — a touristic, but tranquil cóastal resort looking out over the bay. Everyone will enjoy stretching their legs here, and the art lovers among us will surely pay a visit to the Anglada Camarasa museum of oil paintings and Chinese art, opposite the beach at the end of the promenade.

Just before you reached the sea front here at the port, you will have seen the (signposted) PM221 to Formentor branching off left. Return to this road and climb the bare rocky promontory (passing Ⓟ20 at 74km). Several sharp bends later, arrive at the splendidly-engineered **Mirador d'es Colomer★** (78km 📷). A walk along the footpath and up the steps leads to a precipitous viewpoint over the jagged rocks and sea, hundreds of feet below. The rocky Isla Colomer is best seen from here. Opposite the *mirador* steps, a stony path leads up to the old watchtower of Albercutx (Ⓟ21), from where there are unsurpassed views of both Formentor and the Bay of Pollensa.

Down over the other side of the pass now, the PM221 winds between sea and pines towards the magnificent Bay of Formentor, where pale turquoise and aquamarine waters kiss the white sands. Coming to a fork (81km), where a signpost to the **Cape of Formentor** points left, we can continue straight ahead to visit the famous Hotel Formentor, set in exquisite gardens above the beach. This idyllic place was opened in 1926, with a flourish of illuminated advertisements on the Eiffel Tower. The hotel was soon beseiged by the 'jet set' and now many film stars and other VIPs frequent this beautiful paradise by the sea.

Then another eleven kilometres' driving (along a fairly narrow and sometimes vertiginous road with two more *miradors*) brings us to the cape and its lighthouse, poised on the jagged cliffs — the home of Eleanora falcons.

Leaving the beauty of Formentor, we return to the port (116km), and from the seafront, continue ahead to Alcudia (signposted). This is another spectacular drive, following round the bay. At the junction signed Puerto de Alcudia or Palma, we turn left into **Alcudia** town (126km ⚓M✕), once the Roman capital of Mallorca. Originally named 'Pollentia', this thriving Roman city flourished from the second century BC until the sixth century, when it was destroyed by invading Vandals. There are still some remains of the city walls, built during the reign of Jaime II, when the town bore the name of Alcudia, derived from the Moorish word for 'hill'. The museum contains items from Roman times.

Continuing on the C713, we come to traffic lights. Here we can turn right to the **Port of Alcudia** (129km ⚓✕), famous for its freshly-caught lobsters, available in most of the sea-front restaurants. A long, wide beach stretches out into the distance, in front of hotels, sun-clubs and souvenir shops, and the wide marina reaches out into the sea, where ferries from France dock in the deep harbour.

On the way back to the town of Alcudia, be sure to visit the remains of the Roman amphitheatre, on your left, not far outside the town walls (signposted). After your visit, rather than try to turn round in this narrow lane, continue ahead to meet again the C713. Turn right to the traffic lights and then *immediately* left, onto the country road signposted 'Mal Pas' (P22b).

A short drive along this pic- turesque peninsula, through the splendid *urbanización* of Bon Aire (134km ✕) and past the tiny islet of S'Illot (✕), brings us to the turning right to the Ermita de la Victoria (137km ⚓WC✕ P22a). ICONA also provides camping sites in this area, with modern facilities and places for lighting fires.

If you decide to drive the full length of the **Cabo del Pinar**, to Ses Caletes (the 'little coves'), this detour will add 9km to the tour, which returns from the *ermita* back to the traffic lights. Here the C713 offers a straight run of 52km back to Palma (ample ✕🍴). But a final visit is a must: the 8km return detour to the **Cuevas de Campanet★** (P15) is well signposted on the C713. These fabulous underground halls are resplendent with dramatically lighted stalactites and stalagmites. The C713 leads us back to Exit C (203km).

5 THE DELIGHTFUL ORIENT VALLEY

Santa María · Alaró · Orient · Bunyola · Palma

58km/36mi; about 3 hours driving; Exit C from Palma (map p11)

On route: no ✕; Ⓟ3; Walk 3 (and the walk from the PM210 to the Castle of Alaró — brief account below)

A pleasant, short but scenic drive, through olive groves and sheltered valleys — suitable for morning or afternoon

Use the notes for Tour 4 as far as Santa María, where we take the first turning left just as the road widens out in the village centre. This is signposted 'Bunyola'. Pass by an old stone cross in the centre of the road, and then take the first road right (PM202-1, signposted to Alaró). Once out on this quiet country road, you'll drive between almond and carob trees, through landscapes sprinkled with lovely chalets, towards the mountains. Soon the road bends to the right, after which we keep straight ahead, ignoring the various side-roads that lead off to *fincas*. Pass the tiny hamlet of Son Antem (18km), a small cluster of old stone houses. Now the road makes a turn to the left and begins to climb up gradually between the low, pine-covered foothills — an extremely pretty stretch of road — wending its way *tranquilamente* over the undulating landscape (📷 at 20km).

Soon we come into **Alaró** (21km 🍴), an agricultural and industrial village set at the foot of the *sierra*. There isn't a great deal to be seen here, although the old district of the village, where steep and narrow streets weave between the old stone houses, is very picturesque indeed. The PM202-1 curves into the village, passing by the big school on the left, and ends at the main through-road. Turn up to the left here and keep straight on until you see the signpost to Orient on the wall at the end of the street, pointing right. Turn right onto the narrow village street and at the crossroads keep straight on (along the PM210 signposted to Orient).

The narrow road passes between high stone walls, coming into the countryside once again. A great red-rock bluff on our left dominates the landscape, and at 23km a sign indicates the start of the 7km (return) ascent to Alaró Castle atop the bluff. As the total climb is about 600m/1965ft, allow a good three hours for the return walk. The views of the great peaks to the north, setting off the Orient valley and the plain, are magnificent.

The scenic car tour continues through olive orchards and right round the bluff (where you can see the small white chapel up at the top, next to the castle ruins). The road is in good condition, but very narrow in places — don't forget that you *will* meet other cars, though this is not a frequently-used route. Soon, L'Hermitage, a first-class country hotel suddenly comes up on the right (30km ♟♜ ✕) — a good place to 'get away from it all'. And not long after, we begin to see the fairytale village of Orient, set on a rise in the valley below.

Come into **Orient** (32km ♟♟♜✕), nestling at the foot of the Sierra de Alfabia. Park on the main through road, just outside the bar-restaurant, and explore up the old narrow stone steps that lead to the eighteenth-century church. From the church there is a magnificent panorama of pine-clad mountains surrounding the Orient valley, where quaint stone houses crowd together in narrow alleyways down the small hillside. Both of the restaurants in Orient serve the popular Mallorcan dish of *tordos con col*, roast thrushes in cooked cabbage leaves (only available in the winter season; see also page 154). If you're brave enough to try it, it's delicious!

From Orient we continue out of the village on the PM210, now in the direction of Bunyola. Take your time driving through this beautiful, unspoilt valley to enjoy the views of varied landscapes — open farmlands, high mountains and pine forests of unchanging splendour. The road winds up over a low, pine-wooded hill in a series of sharp bends, and then leads down again through the forest, coming gradually into more open countryside.

Then we arrive at **Bunyola** (41km ♟⊕✕℗3), an ancient municipality dating from the time of Jaime I (the Conqueror). Drive on down through the village, keeping to the PM210, until you arrive at the small square and the signpost to Palma. Here you can park and visit the baroque church, as well as one of the many distilleries in the village, where anisette and the typical Mallorcan liqueur, *palo*, are made.

From Bunyola turn right (when coming in from Orient), following the signs to Palma, now along the PM201. Pass by the railway station and continue on for 1km until you meet the C711. Turn left for the straight run (♟ at 57km) in to Exit B in the capital (58km).

(Two kilometres south of Bunyola, a small road leads off right to the Raxa Gardens, which bear comparison with those of Alfabia (Tour 2). If you've time for this detour, the estate is well worth a visit.)

6 VILLAGES OFF THE BEATEN TRACK

Sineu · María de la Salut · Santa Margalida · Ca'n Picafort · La Colonia de San Pedro · Artá · Manacor · Petra · Sant Joan · Algaida · Palma

192km/117mi; about 7 hours driving; Exit D from Palma (map p11)
On route: ✗ at Ca'n Picafort on the C712; Ⓟ4, 23; Walks 4, 23
Although this tour can be completed in a day (not leaving much time for stop-offs), it is ideally a two-day programme. Not all the roads are in first-class condition. Market days are: Wednesday mornings in Sineu (agricultural) and Tuesday afternoons in Ca'n Picafort (touristic)

Leave Palma from the *avenidas* along the Heroes de Manacor (Exit D). Just after the junction, where the ring road crosses, turn left on the PM301-1 in the direction of Sineu (signposted). A fairly uncomplicated run through the countryside, amongst almond orchards and low hills, takes us past Santa Eugenia (Ⓟ4) at 18km. There are some sharp bends to negotiate at about 24km. Past the turning left to Sencelles, our route is renumbered PM314-1 (✗ at 28km).

Come into the agricultural village of **Sineu** (33km ♦✗♨), where we turn left at the 'stop' sign, following the main street through the town. Here on Wednesday mornings a lively open-air agricultural market fills the main square, a tradition kept from as far back as the Middle Ages. People visit from all over the island, and the ambience is one of rural charm. In recent years, however, one or two stalls have been set up to attract tourists, so you can now buy delicate porcelains or copper pots between the vegetables and the livestock. Following along the main thoroughfare, keep left at each fork (♨ at 33.5 km — just down the turn-off to Inca). At the end of the village, you will see a sign to 'María'. Turn right here, and, at the end of this street, turn *right* if you wish to visit the market, or else follow left with us on the PM351 towards María.

This is a pleasant bucolic run over undulating country-side — quite different from the flat lands of the orchards along the Inca road. Pass by a quarry at 36km and soon come to the small country village of **María de la Salut** (40km ♦), completely hidden away from the whirlwinds of tourism. These lands once belonged to the infamous Ramón Zaforteza, whose cruelty earned him the name of the 'Evil Count'. The local church has an interesting Baroque belltower. On entering the village, we turn left, following the signs to Santa Margalida. Then a second left, and, finally a right, brings us to a crossroads at 43km. Here we turn left onto the PM334.

38

Santa Margalida (46km ⚓ — also called Santa Margarita) is set on a low rise and commands excellent views of the distant *sierra* and the plain. Birthplace of the wealthy financier, Juan March, the village still retains some of its past magic — seen in the beautiful old buildings of the ancient rectory and the palace of the Count of Santa María de Formiguera and his family — feudal lords of past, forgotten centuries.

From Santa Margalida, we follow the PM341 to Ca'n Picafort (signposted). The narrow road winds out of the centre and heads for the coast, between plantations of fig trees, carobs, and almond orchards. Keep a sharp lookout for the turning off to Ca'n Picafort (on the right at 52km).

Cross the main C712 (⊼) and come into **Ca'n Picafort** (56km ♨ ✕♨⊕), where a long wide beach stretches out into the distance, below the tiled esplanade. Perhaps you'll stop for a brief thirst-quencher in this popular tourist resort, but soon it's time to press on.

Turn up any of the side streets and head back to the C712, where we make a left turn. The road cuts through shady pine forests and gradually comes out into more open countryside. Soon we pass a turn-off to Son Serra de la Marina, a small coastal urbanisation (68km) and, not long after, a pretty chapel with a belltower appears on the right-hand side of the road, opposite a grand old mansion. Unfortunately, both church and house are usually closed — the owners now residing in Palma — but one can still imagine the splendour of byegone days when elegantly dressed *señoras* would cross over to their private chapel for *misa*.

The continuing C712 passes by the road to Petrá on the right (at 70km) and starts to climb gradually through more pines (♨ at 70.5km). We'll make a detour at 74km: turn left on the PM333-1 out to the **Colonia de San Pedro** (78km ♨✕). The colours of the sea here are unbelievable. There's a small beach in front of the bar-café on the seafront. Let's continue a little further on our detour, along this charming country road, so little visited by tourists. We pass by bright smallholdings and orchards, enclosed by honey-hued dry-stone walls — the rural scene set off all the better by the stark backdrop of the Artá range seen to the south. Soon we come into the charming new *urbanización* of Betlem — reminiscent of Binibeca on Menorca. Perhaps you'll make the time to leave your car at the end of the road and use the notes for Walk 23 (on page 143)

to explore this headland. A short stroll will reward you with splendid views of the Bay of Alcudia to the north and the Artá mountains to the south, dominated by Mount Morey. The iron-rich red rock is populated by pines and innumerable palm bushes, through which beautiful vistas of an aquamarine and indigo sea are framed for your lens.

Returning to the C712, again turn left and climb in a series of bends through the dramatic mountain landscape to **Artá** (96km ⚲✕🍽M), once the private shooting grounds of Jaime II. There is so much to see in Artá, that one really needs to spend an entire afternoon here.

There's a rough sketch-map of the roads radiating from Artá on page 145. To begin, let's take the northernmost road out of the village. This narrow, twisting country lane winds up through desolate hills to the Ermita de Betlem (106km ⚲⛪), set high on the slopes. A cypress-lined avenue leads up to the *ermita*, where you can visit the small chapel. For those who enjoy the solitary peace of these desert-like surroundings, an overnight stay at the hospice is possible (see also pages 61, 155). Up over the brow of the mountain, behind the hermitage buildings, a rocky trail leads to a viewpoint where a magnificent panorama of the wide Bay of Alcudia and the distant rocky peninsula of Formentor unfolds itself before your camera lens, with the Colonia of San Pedro and Betlem below.

Back in Artá town (115km), visit the Almudaina, the site of a Moorish fortress, containing the Sanctuary of San Salvador (visible on entering the town), where parts of the original wall still stand. The archaeological museum is also worth visiting: one of the best on Mallorca, it contains many important pieces, including five bronze statuettes dating from the second century BC. Finally, you won't want to miss the pre-historic site of **Ses Paisses★**, where you can see the *talayots* (towers) of an ancient civilisation. The site is not signposted, but it lies off the Palma—Cala Ratjada road (C715), which is our outgoing route from Artá: to find it, see next-to-last paragraph on page 45.

From Ses Paisses, continue along the C715 (🍽 at 117km) and come into **Sant Llorenç d'es Cardassar** (128km ⚲✕⊕), an ancient feudal village, donated by Jaime I in his attempt to re-populate the area after the Reconquest of Mallorca from the Moors in 1229.

The main road then leads through open countryside to Manacor (136km — described on page 42, Tour 7). Past Manacor and continuing along the C715, we turn right at 140km, onto the PM332. This narrow, pretty country lane brings us to the lonely village of Petra (147km ♦♣M), birthplace of Fray Junípero Serra, the Franciscan friar and missionary to the colonies in North America. He founded many important towns on America's west coast, among them Los Angeles. On entering the village, take the first turning to the left, and then turn left twice more, to reach the small house (Fray Junípero's birthplace) and museum. (To visit, ask for the key at No 15, further along the street.) Not far from here is the seventeenth-century church of the old Franciscan convent of San Bernadino, where Fray Junípero lived for many years while training to become a missionary.

If you wish to visit the sanctuary of Bonany (♦♠), where Fray Junípero preached his last sermon before leaving Mallorca, make a detour back towards the C715 (signed to Palma). The road is met on the right after about 3 km. The hermits here still keep a hospice open to travellers.

Our route leaves Petra on the PM322 and continues to Sant Joan (154km), where one of the most popular *romerías*, the 'Fiesta of Bread and Fishes', is celebrated just before Easter, with special home-made pasties of fish and bread. Apart from this, there's not much of note in the village.

Instead of leaving by the road signposted to Palma, continue through Sant Joan, and turn right, then left, to follow the PM323 towards Sencelles (signposted). A little further along, turn into the PM313-1, to head for Algaida (signposted). By avoiding the C715 for a little longer, we can appreciate the beautiful countryside of this area, not often seen by tourists. The low hills and pine woods soon give way to almond orchards dotted with fig trees.

We rejoin the main road at Algaida (169km ♦✕♣) and from here we have a straight run back to Palma. The road is very good and lined with restaurants, in case you're famished at this point! But if it's not yet too late in the day, you may wish to stop off at the Alorda leather factory★ (at 171km) or the Gordiola glass-blowing factory★ (a little further along, 172km). The road continues past Casa Blanca and Son Ferriol (187km ♣), coming to the outskirts of Palma (♣ at 190km) and entering the city at the point where we began (192km).

7 THE PINE COAST AND THE ARTA CAVES

Manacor · Sant Llorenç · Son Servera · Cala Millor and Cala
Bona · Costa de los Pinos · Canyamel · Cuevas de Artá ·
Capdepera · Cala Ratjada · Cala Guya · Artá · Palma
195km/121mi; about 7 hours driving; Exit D from Palma (map p11)
On route: no X; Ⓟ 24, 25; Walks 24, 25
*You'll need a complete day for this tour, as it's one of the longest.
All the roads are in good condition. Tickets for the Caves of Artá
purchased at the entrance. The caves are open daily (except Christ-
mas day) from 09.00–19.00 (17.00 in winter)*

Exit D from Palma (Heroes de Manacor) becomes the
C715 and takes us directly to Manacor (♨ at 2km and
5km; many ✕), across flat open countryside dotted with
innumerable windmills. Pass **Algaida** (21km ♦✕♨) and then
Montuiri (28km ✕⊕) in a landscape of low hills and pine
woods, cultivated lands and old farmhouses. The road
continues (♨ at 36km) into the village of **Vilafranca de
Bonany** (38km ✕) and then out into rolling countryside
again, until we reach **Manacor** (46km ♠✕♨⊕♦M), the
second industrial town of Mallorca. This is the centre for
hand-carved furniture and the world-famous pearl factory,
Majorica★. Jaime II built himself a palace here, and you
can visit the Torre de Palau, one of the remaining towers
(at the back of the church in the Plaza del Rector Rubí).
This tower houses a small museum, containing prehistoric
objects of bronze and clay (found in cave dwellings in the
hills to the northeast of the town). There are also some
Roman remains, and Moorish ceramics. Manacor's church
is a combination of Gothic origin and neo-Gothic recon-
struction; here, the Municipal Archaeological Museum
contains remnants of mosaics from the paleo-Christian
basilica of Son Peretó near Artá, thought to be part of a
Roman town at the time of Plinius.

Following the road signs to Cala Ratjada, we continue
on the C715 (⊕ at 55km), coming into the agricultural
village of **Sant Llorenç** (55km ♦✕), where we now take the
PM403 to the right. This pretty country lane winds over
low hills, between vegetable gardens and farmlands, into
Son Servera (62km ♦), an ancient municipality — one of the
first districts to be re-populated after the conquest of
Mallorca by Jaime I in 1229. Servera was the name of the
first feudal lord to receive these lands from the hands of
the conquering king. Its economy is now mainly based on
the cultivation of almonds, figs and carobs. We drive into
the village along the narrow street, coming to the square,
where we continue straight ahead.

A signpost to Porto Cristo, Cala Millor, Cala Bona and the Costa de los Pinos indicates a turn to the left, and at the 'give way' sign, we continue along the PM402-3 in the direction of Porto Cristo, coming out into the country again. At 64km, bear left towards Cala Millor (signposted) along the PM402-6 (✘ at 65km). When you come to the crossroads, keep straight ahead on the beautiful tree-lined avenue, soon arriving at **Cala Millor** (66km ♨ ✘⊕), a tourist resort where fine sandy beaches alternate with rocky coves, and hotels, bars and souvenir shops crowd together along the esplanade. Keep straight ahead for the beach, where you may park and explore, or get some refreshment at one of the beach-side cafés.

Or turn left with us, along the sea-front, following the coastal road, which quicky runs into **Cala Bona** (67km ♨ ✘), with its tiny, but very picturesque harbour. We can take any of the turnings up to the left now, to find the (signposted) road to the Costa de los Pinos (the Cape of Pines), where we turn right at the 'stop' sign. Driving along here (✘ at 68, 69, 70km), we pass by many beautiful homes, part of this new *urbanización* built amongst the pines. At 71km come to a road junction; turn right towards the 'Club de Golf', drawing nearer to the sea again (♨ ✘ at 71.5km). Keeping right along the Avenida del Pinar, the road starts to climb up towards the lovely **Costa de los Pinos** (74km 🎦). From the viewpoint we can look down over the Pine Coast, and along to the beaches of Cala Millor and Cala Bona, sheltered by the distant headland that hides Porto Cristo from view.

From the cape we return to the crossroads past the golf club (77km) and take the PM403-2 on the right, signposted to Son Servera. Coming to the first road junction of several (80km), turn right for Capdepera and Artá along a narrower country road (✘ just past the junction). At the next crossroads, again turn right towards Artá (signposted), and, at the 'stop' sign, turn right yet again (✘ at 81km). At the following junction (82km) we keep straight on towards Capdepera, leaving the road to Artá on the left. We're now on the PM404, a very pretty country route that runs over low hills and through pine woods. We'll soon have to negotiate a series of tight bends over the last hill, where a large signpost welcomes us on behalf of the region of Capdepera. The road twists on down the opposite side of the hill, with some excellent views across the countryside.

Meeting a crossroads at 86km, we turn right on the PM404-2 towards Canyamel (signposted), passing by the

Torre de Canyamel (87km ✕), a square tower built during the fourteenth century over Arab and Roman foundations, and where the country people were able to take refuge during pirate sieges. Not long ago, this tower was converted into a museum, but unfortunately it is now closed, although the restaurant is still open. Continue on towards the coast, turning left at the roundabout (90km), towards the **Playa de Canyamel** (91km ♨ ✕). This is an exceptionally pretty bay with a fine sandy beach, protected on either side by high cliffs and bordered by pines — another 'get away from it all' place! Turning back to the roundabout, we double back on our tracks past the Tower of Canyamel, to take the turning on the right towards the Caves of Artá (signposted). Following along here on the PM404-2, we begin to climb above the beach at Canyamel and then find the entrance to **Las Cuevas de Artá★** (100km ☎).

A long stone stairway leads up into the enormous dark hole in the rock cliff. Tickets are purchased by the bar at the entrance; then we begin our fantastic journey into the caves, once the hideout of bands of pirates. The visit lasts for about three-quarters of an hour, and we go deep down into the eerie chambers — where we are silently greeted by the Queen of Stalagmites, reaching up 22m/70ft, in the 'room of a thousand columns'. From here we're led into the Inferno, where from the *mirador* we are mesmerised by music coming from the depths in a *son et lumière* spectacle of devilry and strange lights. Coming up out of Purgatory, we pass through a series of stone bridges, stairways and tunnels, visiting the 'theatre', the Lamp Room and the Flag Chamber, before finally coming up into Paradise, where an 'organ' and an 'angel's wings' can be seen on the walls of the huge chamber. Later, the Diamond Stone and the Ghost bid us a mute farewell, and we come blinking up into the daylight, where a stark and dazzling blue sea reflects the bright sunlight of the outside world.

We return to the PM404-2, heading in the direction of Artá, but at the next road junction (104km), we turn right towards Capdepera and Cala Ratjada (signposted). At the following crossroads we take the PM404 on the right to **Capdepera** (107km ⸱ ✕), where a medieval fortress and walls crown the top of the hill. You can visit the small oratory inside the walls, built by King Sancho during the fourteenth century, and a walk around the parapets gives a magnificent panorama of the bay at Cala Ratjada and the pine-wooded coast.

From Capdepera we continue along the main through road towards Cala Ratjada and Cala Guya. Taking the C715 towards the left, we soon come into the tourist resort of **Cala Ratjada** (110km ♙♨×⚓⊕). The picturesque little fishing port and the lighthouse merit a visit (keep straight ahead where the narrow road twists up the side of the cliff above the coast (111km ☜)). The views from here are wonderful: endless sea and pines and rocky cliffs. Returning to the centre, turn right just before the church for **Cala Guya** (also called — and signposted — Cala Agulla); there's a sketch map on page 148. A short run between hotels and restaurants quicky leads to an idyllic, half-moon beach (114km), where we can explore over the sand dunes or make a short walk to Es Guyó or the Coll de Marina (℗25).

Once again in Cala Ratjada, we follow the signs into the village centre and out into the countryside along the C715, towards Artá, bypassing Capdepera and the road to Cala Estreta (℗24) up right at 125km.

There's not enough time today to visit **Artá** (127km ↕×⚓M — see Tour 6) properly, but there may be time enough for a visit to the prehistoric village of **Ses Paisses★**, with its megalithic stone 'towers' (*talayots*). The site is not signposted: continue on the C715 towards Palma and, *at the first bend*, take the turning across to the left — just by a small thatched hut, crossing the railway line and then driving down the narrow lane for about 1km (129km).

Our excursion ends by following the outgoing route back to Palma, again past the countless windmills, now silhouetted against the setting sun. We come into the city by Exit D after 195km.

8 LAS CALAS DE MALLORCA

Campos · Felanitx · Cala Murada · Las Calas de Mallorca · Cuevas del Drach · Porto Cristo · S'Illot · Safari Park · Palma

171km/106mi; about 6 hours driving; Exit E from Palma (map p11)

On route: no X; no P, but Las Calas de Mallorca offer excellent picnicking; no Walks

This excursion makes a full day's programme. Roads are good, but you'll want to spend ample time at a few spectacular stop-offs! Tickets are available at the gates for:

Caves of Drach (Porto Cristo): open 11.00–12.00 and 14.00–15.00 summer (Saturdays 12.00–14.00 only); open 12.00–14.00 winter

Aquarium, Porto Cristo: open 09.30–19.00 daily

Hams Caves (not included in our tour): open 10.00–17.00 daily

AutoSafari Park of Son Servera: open 09.00–19.00 daily

L as Calas de Mallorca, or The Mallorcan Coves, consist of a series of tiny bays and inlets, some with sandy beaches, just below Porto Cristo. The coves are strung out along a picturesque stretch of wild and rocky coastline. Later in the day, our tour takes in two other tourist attractions: the beautiful Caves of Drach, where you'll take a silent boat ride across an underground lake, and an unforgettable safari through an African animal reserve.

We take the motorway (Exit E from Palma), in the direction of Santanyí, turning left onto the C717 at 8.5km. The route cuts through pines and almond orchards (❦ at 11km, X at 15km) and comes directly into the market town of **Lluchmayor** (23km X❦; see Tour 10). We then cross rolling countryside (❦ at 26km) before reaching **Campos** (36km X❦ see Tour 10). In Campos, we leave the C717, turning left onto the PM512 to Felanitx (signposted). Crossing open countryside and cultivated farmlands, we arrive at the large town of **Felanitx** (47km ♠ X❦⊕♦), a wine-making centre, also noted for its thriving ceramics industry. The church is built in the same honey-coloured stone as Palma's cathedral.

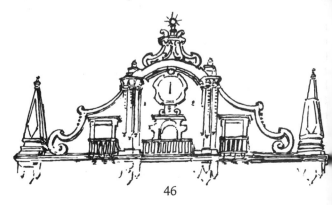

In the centre, we cut across town by the rather complicated one-way traffic system, down narrow streets, keeping a *very* sharp lookout for the signpost to 'Porto Colom' at the exit from Felanitx. We now travel on the countryside PM401, going round a small roundabout and continuing straight on, passing by a side road on the right which leads to the Sanctuary of San Salvador (Tour 9).

Carrying on through a landscape of low, pine-covered hills, we must begin to look for the road (PM401-4) to Cala Murada (signposted), which turns off to the left just by the side of a country restaurant (57km ✕). Follow this road for 2km, and then turn right (59km), through pine woods, into **Cala Murada** (62km ♙ ✕). Driving as far as the sea front, we discover a pleasant — not too large — sandy beach, just below the rocky headland; this popular beach is often crowded, especially at the height of the season.

Returning to the PM401-4, we now turn right, passing side roads leading down to small coves and tourist apartments. The road to Cala Domingos comes up next on our right (66km), in case you'd like to visit. The country road rambles on (✕ at 67km) over the low hills, mostly covered in scrubs and sparsely populated by pines. A series of bends leads us to the turn-off to the Coves of Mallorca (69km). Turn right and first pass a rather desolate-looking area, with a scattering of new hotels sitting ostentatiously on the rocks and looking terribly out of place. Here a multitude of stony tracks criss-cross down to the various coves of the **Calas de Mallorca** (73km ♙ ✕). The small rocky bays are certainly picturesque and provide very good picnic spots. Park your car and walk over the headlands, discovering the different *calas*, where small beaches hide amongst the rocks along this wild part of the Mallorcan shore. Paths lead from one cove to another, and the colours of the sea vary from the palest turquoise to deep blues and greens.

Returning to the main route (PM401-4), we again turn right; now the pine-clad hills are interspersed with almond orchards along this stretch. Soon a turning to the right (84km) takes us to the pretty cove of Cala Romántica (85km ✕), another smallish inlet with a beautiful sandy beach in romantic surroundings, as its name implies. Again turn right, after rejoining the main northeasterly route, still making for Porto Cristo.

At 93km, just outside Porto Cristo, we turn right into the road to the fabulous **Cuevas del Drach★**. The Archduke Luis Salvador (see also pages 25 and 79) commissioned the French geologist, Martel, to explore and map out these wonderful caves, which the Archduke had discovered on his very extensive travels all over the island. Our visit will take about one hour: the guided tour goes through a labyrinth of stone passageways, steps and caverns — brilliantly and cleverly illuminated — where a magical world of coloured stalagmites and stalactites and the crystal waters of underground lakes create a dreamlike atmosphere. Finally, a mystical boat journey across the underground Martel Lake (177m/580ft long and very deep indeed) brings our dream to an end, and we leave the caves, coming up out into the stark daylight of reality. Unfortunately, no photography is permitted inside the caves.

Returning again to the main route, almost at once we are in the coastal resort of **Porto Cristo** (95km ▲ ✕), an ancient fishing port for many centuries. It is thought that this was also an important seaport during Roman times. The excellent aquarium overlooking the harbour is worth a visit, as are the Hams Caves, if you can afford the time.

Continuing straight ahead through the town centre, we follow the signs to Son Servera, turning right just in front of the memorial cross (Porto Cristo was the only Mallorcan village to suffer badly in the Civil War). The PM402-3 to Son Servera soon brings us to the turning off right to **S'Illot** (97km ▲✕), a beautiful holiday resort boasting a wide and sandy beach. Carry on through S'Illot and then take the road opposite Cala Moreya up left to rejoin the main route (102km ✕).

It's now just over a kilometre to the turning right for the **AutoSafari Park of Son Servera★** (105km). A slow drive along the arrowed route through this African animal reserve gives good views of rhinos, elephants, giraffes, zebras . . . in their natural surroundings. Do beware of the mischevious apes, ready to make off with your picnic leftovers or camera cases! It's a good idea to keep the windows of your car closed. There's also an aquarium here, well worth a visit before you leave the park.

From the 'Reserva Africana' we return to Porto Cristo, where we keep to the right, in front of the memorial cross, in the direction of Manacor. At the end of the road, we turn right again at the 'stop' sign (112km), along the PM402 (✿ at 113km, ✕ at 120km). This road passes the entrance to the Hams Caves. In **Manacor** (123km ✕✿; description Tour 7) we turn left and then right, towards the square, following the signs to Palma. Finally, coming out into the C715, a straight run across the countryside (ample ✕✿), brings us back to Palma's *avenidas* at Exit D, after 171km.

Santanyí · Cala Figuera · Porto Petro · Cala d'Or · Porto
Colom · Felanitx · Santuario de San Salvador · Castell de
Santueri · Porreres · Palma

188km/117mi; about 7 hours driving; Exit E from Palma (map p11)

On route: ✗ at San Salvador; no ℗ or walks — but the calas *offer
splendid picnicking opportunities*

*The best time of year for this tour is spring and early summer; it fits
well into a leisurely one-day programme, with ample time for stops*

Vastly different from the mountainous regions of the
western coastline, Mallorca's eastern coast consists of
a series of small coves, where tourist resorts have sprung up
in recent years, burgeoning side-by-side with extensive
agricultural centres.

Leave Palma on the motorway (Exit E), using the notes
on page 46 (Tour 8) as far as Campos. But today there's
time to make a brief stop-off on the outskirts of Lluchmayor, at the 'Molí d'En Gaspar', an old windmill converted
into a museum. You'll pass it on the C717, just outside the
town.

From **Campos** (36km ✗🅐; see Tour 10), we continue on
the C717 through open countryside (🅐 at 38.5km) and soon
come into the village of **Santanyí** (50.5km ✗🅐⊕🅐), set in
some five kilometres from the east coast. Do not leave the
C717 yet, but keep on ahead, entering the ancient fortified
town, dominated by its church. From the village, *carefully*
follow the signposts to Cala Figuera, to join the PM610-2.

This country road comes out of Santanyí and into an
open landscape, passing a smaller side road off to Cala
Santanyí on the right. The road is wide here, and soon the
tang of fresh sea breezes announces our arrival at one
of the prettiest coves in Mallorca, **Cala Figuera** (56km 🏠 ✗),

49

where we turn left for the picturesque little fishing port ensconced amongst the pine trees. Drive down the little road, between chalets and attractive villas, to where a deep channel of blue sea reflects the scenic fishing port like a watery oil painting. You can park anywhere along here, and stroll along the rocky promontory to watch the various fishing boats chugging out to the open sea, or to take photographs against a background of jagged rocks, the scene of many an onslaught by pirates and Saracens in past centuries.

To continue our route to Porto Petro, we must first go back to Santanyí, where we follow the signs towards Cala d'Or through the village. We rejoin the C717 for a short time, passing a small side road up left (at 66km) that leads up to the Sanctuary of the Consolation, a small oratory built during the 17th century. Not long after, we come into the hamlet of **Alquería Blanca** (68km ♟). Continue ahead, taking a left at the next signposting towards Cala d'Or, but keep a sharp lookout for the road to Porto Petro which soon comes up on the right. Turn right on this (signposted) road (✕ at 70km) and come into **Porto Petro** (73km ♟♠✕), a small fishing village reminiscent of Porto Cristo (Tour 8). You can sit here by the still waters of the harbour, under the colourful awnings of the bar-cafés, and watch the world go by for a little while.

From Porto Petro we can go directly to Cala d'Or: good signposting indicates the short coastal route. First we come into the tiny harbour of Cala Llonga, part of **Cala d'Or** (77km ♠✕). You'll need time to explore this 'Golden Cove'. There's a truly beautiful beach, where the sea is an unbelievable shade of palest turquoise — patched with royal blue, and rocky inlets of aquamarine waters bite into the coast.

Find the road to Palma coming out of Cala d'Or, and follow the signs to Cala Ferrera next, coming to a roundabout, from where we continue along the Avenida Cala Ferrera. Cala Ferrera (80km ♠✕), Cala Serena (81km ♠✕) and Cala Esmeralda are smaller — but equally beautiful — coves adjoining Cala d'Or; visit them if you have time.

From Cala Serena we head for Porto Colom (signposted) on a narrow country lane across open farmlands dotted with almond orchards and bordered by dry-stone walls. Meet the PM401-2 at S'Horta, and here turn right for Porto Colom. A couple of kilometres along, turn right for the port, through a landscape of pines and low scrubs, sprinkled with villas. Come into **Porto Colom** (93km ♠✕).

a centuries-old important commercial port, now also a beautiful residential area and summer resort. Visit the lighthouse, following the signs to 'Es Tancat de Sa Torre', from where you will capture some excellent views of the coast, or find the pretty little cove of Cala Marsal, hiding between the cliffs.

Leaving Porto Colom, we make for Felanitx on the PM401 (✗☂ at 104km). Pine woods and almond orchards cover low hills, and the mountain of San Salvador can be seen ahead on the left. At 113km, turn into the smaller road on the left, the PM404-1, where you will see the signpost to the Sanctuary of San Salvador. The road soon starts to climb the mountainside, winding through thick pine woods to the hermitage.

Many sharp bends later, we arrive at the **Santuario de San Salvador** (116km ♦♠✗✗☺) at a height of 510m/1675ft. There's ample parking, so let's unpack our picnics and explore the wonderful panorama below us, a truly magnificent landscape of Mallorca. On clear days, much of the eastern coast is visible, with the mountains of Artá floating on the clouds to the north, and the distant *sierra* closing the western horizon. Porto Colom appears like a small toy port on the coast, and the town of Felanitx lies silently below the *puig* like an uninhabited miniature world. A high, impressive monument to Jesus Christ dominates the hilltop in front of the car park. It stands 37m/120ft high, and the actual figure, sculpted by Francisco Salvá, measures a full 7 metres (23ft). The crypt underneath contains the remains of five hermits — and of the man who paid for the monument. The sanctuary itself was first built around the year 1348, after Pedro IV of Aragon gave his permission, with the condition that at each mass, prayers would be said for him and all of his successors. In 1595 a second temple was built, and during the seventeenth century, this also served as an *atalaya* (see page 153), communicating with the other watchtowers at Porto Colom, Montesión and Santanyí. A third building was constructed during the eighteenth century, although the actual guest rooms were not added until later; the dates can be seen on the walls. A hostelry is still run by the monks, although they do not encourage brief overnight stays (see also pages 61 and 155). The chapel is interesting for its thirteenth-century Madonna statue and the beautiful Gothic altarpiece.

Leaving the sanctuary, we return by the hairpin bends to the main road, turning left on the PM401, and coming into **Felanitx** (122km ✗☂, see Tour 8). Enter the town and keep straight ahead, passing by the municipal park along the Calle Bellpuig and coming to the square. Continue ahead, to turn left later along the Calle Major, looking for the signposts to Palma. Come to a second square, decorated by elegant palms, where we continue ahead. Then we see the signposts to Santanyí, along the Calle Santueri (C714). Follow this route now, to visit the remains of the thirteenth-century castle of Santueri.

A small side road leads off left at 126km, signed 'Castell de Santueri'. The narrow tarmac lane winds through almond and fruit orchards, orange groves and vineyards (✕ at 129km), and then curves up to the castle (131km). (In the winter, stop at the large house on the second bend to ask for the key.) This castle was reconstructed over the remains of an ancient Arab stronghold during the thirteenth century. It is said that a Mussulman held out for eighteen months here, after the invasion of Mallorca by Jaime I, and it is easy to see how this could be possible! Built in a very strategic position, the stronghold rested on the top of an isolated mountain with steep drops on all sides. There is not, unfortunately, anyone to guide us, and visitors are left to their own devices. The views are, once again, very captivating.

Now we return to Felanitx (137km), from where we follow the signs to Porreres and Palma. Enter the town as far as the first 'stop' sign, to find the Porreres/Palma signs. We join the PM510, and passing by the stone cross monument, head into the countryside towards Porreres. The road traverses many vineyards and flat cultivated lands.

Come into **Porreres** (151km ♦✖). From here, you may wish to make a seven kilometre detour to the Sanctuary of Montesión (♦♠✕⌂). If so, follow the signs for Lluchmayor, which bring you to the PM502 leading southwest out of the village. The road to the sanctuary is met on the left, almost at once. Like other island hermitages, it is beautifully sited, commanding ideal views, and provides food and lodging in simple surroundings (see also pages 61 and 155).

Our itinerary, however, now makes for Palma. The route is well signed in Porreres, and we join the PM503, passing the petrol station and making for open countryside. At the crossroads, in front of the 'Ermita de la Cruz' (153km ♦), turn right in the direction of Montuiri. At the 'stop' sign (C715) turn left and make for Palma, passing **Montuiri** (✕⊕), **Algaida** (♦✕) and ample petrol stations and restaurants, as well as the Alorda leather factory★ and the Gordiola glass-blowing factory★. Enter Palma at Exit D (188km).

10 THE SOUTH AND THE PUIG DE RANDA

El Arenal · Cala Blava · Cabo Blanco · Capocorp Vey · S'Estanyol · Ses Covetes · Es Trenc · La Colonia de San Jordi · Campos · Lluchmayor · Puig de Randa and Santuario de Cura · Palma

147km/91mi; about 6 hours driving; Exit E from Palma (map p11)
On route: ☓ at Cura; no ℗ or walks; good picnicking at the coves
Another all-day tour, ideally for summer, since it includes some of the island's most beautiful and unspoilt beaches. We end up at the Puig de Randa, from where the whole of this itinerary is captured in one magnificent view of the southeast coastline

Driving right down to the eastern end of Palma's *avenidas*, keep left for the turning onto the motorway (Exit E), signposted for the airport and Santanyí. Continue along, past the airport turnoff, as far as the sign for 'Playa de Palma', where we leave the motorway for **Ca'n Pastilla** (7.5km ♠ ✕♙⊕). This is the beginning of the extensive sandy beach and tourist area of **El Arenal** (♠✕⊕). At the traffic lights (♙ to the right), keep straight ahead, as far as the sea-front, and follow this alongside the promenade, where an endless chain of hotels, bar-cafés and swimming pools borders the left-hand side of the road. Countless traffic lights and numbered *balnearios* are our constant companions along here. When we reach the other end of the bay, we turn to the left (by the sign to 'Cabo Blanco'), up a steep hill bordered by souvenir shops and yet more hotels. A road junction is met at the top. Here, at the 'give way' sign, take the second turning on the right, in the direction of Cala Blava (signposted). The PM601-4 finally takes us to the end of this conglomeration of hotels, restaurants and night-clubs, and escapes into the countryside between low pines and scrub.

But it's not long before we reach the urbanisation of **Cala Blava** (15km ♠✕) on the right, where modern villas and low blocks of holiday apartments fringe the small beach. This is our last view of the sea for some kilometres; from now on cliffside roads carry us to S'Estanyol. The PM601-4 continues towards Cabo Blanco, soon passing a turn-off to another recent housing development, **Las Palmeras** (17km ♠✕), on the left. The road from here crosses a rather desolate landscape of rough terrain and low scrub, where neither agriculture nor the frenetic pace of tourism have yet disturbed Nature (save for ♠✕ at 19.5km). A third urbanisation, Bahía Azul, comes up like an oasis in the desert at 22km (✕), after which the sporadic presence of some pines begins to add more colour to the landscape.

Soon the road nears the coast again, running alongside the high cliff-tops on the right, and it will not be long before we're at **Cabo Blanco** (31km 🖼). From this 'white cape', there are excellent views of a wild, desolate part of Mallorca's coast. Then the road swings inland, passing by the military quarters, and heads once more for open country. Pass by the turn-off to Cala Pí (🏨✕), a small resort set in a creek, and almost at once come to one of the most important prehistoric sites in the Balearics, at **Capocorp Vey★** (36.5km).

The gates to the site are padlocked, but ask for the key at the old farmhouse across the road, where the custodian lives. You'll also be given an explanatory pamphlet. Excavations made here uncovered many important archaeological pieces, such as pottery, bone implements and grindstones, supporting the theory that prehistoric peoples lived in this settlement from about 3000 years ago up until Roman times. Unfortunately, the 'finds' have been taken to the Archaeological Museum in Barcelona. But a scramble over the megalithic blocks permits examination of the many chambers, where silence floods through the dry-stone doorways, evoking scenes of a bronze-age community grinding their wheat and tending their fires.

Back on the move, we continue in the direction of S'Estanyol (✕ at 37.5km), bypassing the road right to Vallgornera and turning right on the PM601-5. Enter the not very exciting resort of **S'Estanyol** (48km ✕) and keep on down to the sea front. Here turn left for La Rapita, a small seaside place further along the coast, where many Mallorcan families (mostly from the Lluchmayor region) spend their summer holidays. The main road through **La Rapita** (✕ at 52km) leads away from the sea, but we take a side road off right at 53km, signposted 'Ses Covetes'. This narrow country lane meanders between old stone farms houses where prickly-pear cacti ramble at random, for about another kilometre; then we turn right once more, driving through pines to the coast.

Come to **Ses Covetes** (56km ✕), and for the beach, turn right along the sandy 'road' at the end. Here, a stretch of white sand and clear blue waters extends into the far distance, and, just by the small rocky headland, a beach-side kiosk offers good, cheap meals (in summer). We can also explore from here the fabulous, long white beach of **Es Trenc** (signposted). Turning back in the car, it's a short drive over the unsurfaced track between sand dunes to this lovely beach. It's surely one of the most beautiful on Mallorca — kilometres of unspoilt sand and sea, edged by dunes, and as yet untouched by tourism. Here there's some peace and respite from the usual touristic scene of the island's more popular resorts. Further along Es Trenc, nudists bathe in the natural surroundings of this paradisial beach.

Head back to the asphalted road and turn right. At the junction one kilometre further on, keep straight ahead, through open farmlands, until you reach the 'stop' sign (✕), and there turn right. At the next crossroads, turn right again, back onto the PM601-4 (63km), which takes us through more cultivated lands. Along here, we come to various crossroads: at the first (66km), keep straight ahead, in the direction of Ses Salines (signposted), and at the second (68.5km), turn right onto the PM604, towards the Colonia de San Jordi (signposted). Some pine trees now break the monotony of the flat landscape (♠ at 70km).

To the right we see the salt pans and great white 'mountains' of salt. This is a rich and important ecological centre of the island, where ornithologists are in their element and can observe a variety of aquatic and migratory birds — including herons, sandpipers, ospreys, the rarer flamingoes, and sometimes even kingfishers.

At the next road junction, turn right once again to come into the **Colonia de San Jordi** (74km ♠✕♞). Take the left-hand fork, on reaching the petrol station, towards the picturesque port and the small pine-shaded beach, accessible only on foot.

Leaving the colony behind, we turn back up the main road (right from the petrol station), to follow the PM610 briefly. But turning left at the second road junction, following signs to Campos, we continue along the PM604 (✕ at 82km), until we reach the C717. Here turn left and into **Campos** (91km ♠✕♞).

Designated *villa* as early as 1300, no less than five watch-towers were built in Campos in the fourteenth century. Drive straight into the village, passing to the left of the petrol station, and continuing along the main thoroughfare, where you'll come to the church. Should you wish to visit it (key available in the neighbouring house), art lovers will be able to admire a painting by Murillo, which originally hung in the Sant Blai hermitage not far from the village. Apart from this, Campos is basically an agricultural village and does not have a great deal to offer the passing tourist. Leaving Campos on the C717, continue on in a westerly direction through orchards and cultivation.

Soon we come into **Lluchmayor** (104km ✕🍴🛏M). The eighteenth-century church and the seventeenth-century Convent of Buenaventura are the main architectural high-

lights, while on the outskirts of the village (on the C717 to Palma) a stone cross indicates the site of a confrontation between the troops of Jaime III and the army of Pedro IV of Aragón. You might also take this opportunity to visit the small museum in an old windmill called 'Es Molí d'En Gaspar', on the C717 just *before* you come into the town of Lluchmayor.

Today's tour leaves the centre of the village on the PM501, where we follow the signs to Algaida. This is a picturesque country road that leads through pine-wooded hills and orchards. Soon the road to Randa comes up on the right (at 109km). Drive into the small hamlet set at the foot of the Puig de Randa, an isolated massif standing out from the central plain.

In **Randa** (109.5km 🛏✕), driving slowly along the narrow street, find the signpost for the 'Santuario de Cura', following round to the left and then sharply up right on the PM501-8. The road starts to tackle the mountainside in a series of tight bends, climbing up through pines. Not very far along are the wide gates to the Santuario de Gracia (111km 🛏📷), founded in the Middle Ages, and once a hostelry. Set under the brow of an enormous scarp, the spot is certainly worth a visit, if just to admire the beautiful tiling in the small chapel. The views are already splendid just this far up the road, but we keep climbing, passing by another small oratory on the right — this one dedicated to San Honorato.

Finally, at a height of 548m/1800ft, we arrive at the **Santuario de Cura** (115km ♦♠M✕⬚). Leave the car in the ample parking area outside the sanctuary walls and enter a wide courtyard. Visits to the library and small chapel are a must. The ancient library contains many manuscripts, prayer books and other relics from the days of the thirteenth-century scholar, Ramon Llull, who was born shortly after Jaime I conquered Mallorca.

Apart from the historical value of the visit, there are glorious views in all directions from atop this *puig*: the southern coastline is clearly visible all the way to Palma, reaching down to Cabo Blanco and along to the Cape of Salinas, where a millpond-like Mediterranean caresses the shore. The island of Ibiza floats magically on a blue horizon on clear days, and the rocky offshore isle of Cabrera can also be seen. The long chain of the Sierra de Tramuntana rides on the opposite horizon, to the north, and the wide central plain stretches out below, dotted with countless towns and hamlets. On a clear day, Alcudia's bay is visible from here as well.

A hostelry has been run for many years here at Cura; anyone can spend the night (see also pages 61, 155). Cura is also a popular place for wedding receptions — as you'll see from the display of photos in the bar-restaurant.

We wind back down the mountain, and from Randa, we turn right for Algaida on the PM501. Coming into the large village of **Algaida** (125km ♦✕), keep left, following the signs to Palma. Joining the C715 at 127km, we head left for the capital, following the route described on page 41 and coming into Exit D, the Heroes de Manacor, at 147km.

Walking

This book covers about 250km — 150 miles — of some of the best walking on Mallorca. I can't claim that *all* the best walks have been included; some classic climbs in the northeast — for instance Mount Galatzó — have been omitted in favour of spanning a wider territory. I hope in this way to give walkers a better feeling for the great variety of island landscapes — pastoral byways, as well as dramatic panoramas.

I hope you'll also use this book, together with the bus, train and boat timetables on pages 159-161 to make up your own walk combinations: I've indicated where routes link up on the walking maps, and the large colour map shows the general location of all the walks. One word of caution: **Never try to get from one walk to another on uncharted terrain!** Only link up walks by following paths described in these notes or by using roads or tracks: don't try to cross rough country (which might prove dangerous) or private land (where you may not have right of way).

There are walks in the book for everyone:

Beginners: Start on the walks graded 'easy', and be sure to check all the short and alternative walks — some are easy versions of the long walks for experts.

Experienced walkers: If you are used to rough terrain and have a head for heights, you should be able to tackle all the walks in the book (except those labelled Ⓖ) — taking into account, of course, the weather conditions and their consequences. For example, if it has been raining recently, some of the mountain walks will be unsuitable. Also, storm damage can make the way unsafe at any time. Remember, too, always to follow the route as described in this book. If you have not reached one of the landmarks after a reasonable time, you must go back to the last 'sure' point and start again.

Experts: You should not need a guide for any of the walks, provided you are used to sheer, unprotected drops and always use extreme caution.

Guides, waymarking, maps

Some of the walks are labelled Ⓖ, and I recommend that anyone except an *expert* walker hire a guide for these routes. This is because some areas are prone to sudden, thick mists, making it easy to get lost on a mountain; or because the path is hazardous, or difficult to distinguish, due to the lack of good waymarking.

Guides are not easily found on Mallorca, but you can enquire at Palma's Tourist Promotion Office, 1 Avenida Constitución. Alternatively, you can write in advance or telephone to Mauricio Espinar, Calle Almirante Cervera 23, Puerto de Pollensa (Tel: 531030). He can guide you over any part of the island; he speaks fluent English and French and understands some German.

Waymarking of walks is minimal. There is no signposting, but many of the mountain routes have been marked with red paint in years past (often hard to follow today). Another form of waymarking you'll see on the more difficult mountain routes is the small pile of stones — after a while, you'll become accustomed to keeping a keen eye out for these unusual mountain 'signs'.

The **maps** in this book have been heavily adapted from 1:50,000 and 1:25,000 military maps of the island. These are available in Palma at No 76, Calle Arzobispo Aspargo, should you wish to pursue more walks. But do remember that, while they are useful for contours and heights, they are woefully out of date, and the routes shown may now be completely overgrown and dangerous — or privately owned.

R ight of way

Much of Mallorca's land is in private hands, and several landowners do try to discourage walkers by posting forbidding 'private' signs.* There are no maps showing rights of way either. But, by law, walkers have right of way to: the coast, famous landmarks, *miradors*, monasteries and hermitages, towers and mountain peaks. You do have the right of way on all the routes described in this book, but should you encounter any difficulty with a landowner, do tell him just *where* you are going. The landowner might ask:

'A dónde van?' (sounds like: ah **dohn**-deh **vahn**; means: 'Where are you going?').

To which you should reply:

'Nos vamos a ...' (nohs **vah**-mos ah — 'We're going to ...'), followed by the landmark in the walk. It may be that you have strayed off the main path of the walk, in which case he can redirect you (see also the language hints on page 158).

*'Coto privado de caza' simply means private *hunting* — ignore it!

Dogs and other things that bite

You'll encounter **dogs** at all the farms, *almost* always chained up. It is a good idea for each walker always to carry a stout stick — to be used for self-protection; but when passing through a farm *never* wave the stick about to menace the dogs. Moreover, always go *quietly* through all private land, leaving gates *exactly* as you find them. Only resort to your stick when confronted by an unchained and obviously unfriendly dog.

There are four types of **snakes** on the island — some of the longest growing to about 1–1.5m (1–1½yds); none are dangerous to man. We also have **scorpions**, but these are tiny (4cm/1½in). Their bite might sting, but you won't come to any harm. More troublesome are **mosquitos** and **tics**. Always carry insect repellant, and when walking in dense undergrowth, it's always wise to wear long trousers, with your socks pulled up round the trouser legs, and long sleeves.

Walkers' checklist

The following points cannot be stressed too often:

- At any time a walk may become **unsafe** due to heavy storms. If the route is not as described in this book, and your way ahead is not secure, do not attempt to go on.
- Walks labelled Ⓖ are generally unsuitable for winter walking, and the walks in the mountains *may* be very wet in winter — although not necessarily so.
- Never walk alone — four is the best walking group.
- Do not overestimate your energies — your speed will be determined by the slowest walker in your group.
- Transport connections at the end of a walk are vital.
- Proper shoes or boots are a necessity.
- Mists can suddenly appear on the higher mountains.
- Warm clothing is needed on the mountains; even in summer take some along, just in case you are delayed.
- Compass, whistle, torch weigh little, but might save your life.
- Extra rations must be taken on long walks.
- Always take a sunhat with you, and in summer a cover-up for your arms and legs as well.
- A stout stick is a help on rough terrain and to discourage the rare unchained, menacing dog.
- Do not panic in an emergency.
- Read and re-read the important note on page 2 and the country code on page 64, as well as guidelines on grade and equipment for each walk you plan to make.

Where to stay

Most people will be staying in or around Palma during their holiday on the island. From the capital a good public transport system permits daily travel to most parts of Mallorca. For this reason, all the walks are written up to include transport to and from Palma, where there is a wide selection of accommodation.

Whereas the capital is your best choice if you're relying on public transport, if you plan to rent a car you have a far greater choice of locations — especially if you plan only to make short or easy walks.

If you intend to do a lot of hiking, remember that most of the island's best — and most strenuous — walks lie along the mountain chain stretching from Valldemossa to Pollensa. Good centres for walks are therefore Soller and its port and Pollensa and its port. This is especially so when the bus is running along the C710 mountain road between Soller and Pollensa (see STOP PRESS, page 168); many of the walks then lie within easy reach.

Briefly, if you're planning to make a lot of walks, are *pre-booking a package holiday*, and will rely on public transport, **Palma** is your best centre. **Pollensa** and **Soller** are also good choices, especially if the C710 bus is running.

For those *not* booking 'all-in' holidays, there is the interesting alternative of staying at one of Mallorca's sanctuaries, many of which still run a hostelry.

Lluc, a large monastery, steeped in history and set in romantic surroundings high in the mountains, is placed just at the centre of some of the best island walks. Visitors may stay overnight — or for as long as they wish — in the hostelry run by the friars. A bus service connects Lluc with Inca, from where there are hourly trains to Palma — so there's no need to feel 'cut off from civilisation'. Moreover, if the bus is running along the C710 between Soller and Pollensa, passing by Lluc — see page 168 — this hostelry becomes even more appealing as a centre.

The next best base for hostelry accommodation is Pollensa, where a small sanctuary atop the **Puig de María** (Walk 18) offers modest and inexpensive accommodation in spotless rooms with breathtaking views. A number of other sanctuaries take in visitors, among them the Ermita de Betlem in the Artá mountains, the Ermita de la Victoria near Alcudia, the Ermita de la Trinidad near Valldemossa, the Monastery of Cura (Randa), the Sanctuary of San Salvador (Felanitx) and the Sanctuary of Montesión (Porreres) — but of these, only the first three are near to our walks.

Weather

The weather on Mallorca can be quite variable. It can be very cold in winter — but not necessarily so. In fact, some winters are pleasantly mild. It is swelteringly hot and humid from July to September. The most unreliable months are March/April and September/October, when the capricious spring and autumn rains arrive.

Most people will find it far too hot in summer for any of the strenuous walks in this book. There are only two walks in the book which *must* be made in summer: Walk 8, from the Mirador de Ses Barques to La Calobra, relies on a boat connection from La Calobra, and this generally operates only between May and September. This walk is not too strenuous, especially if you omit the descent and return from Sa Costera. But there is very little shade; be sure to wear a sunhat and something covering your arms and the back of your neck and legs, and take plenty of water or fruit with you. Walk 9 (along the Torrente de Pareis) is only possible in summer, or after a long period without rain; it also relies on the La Calobra boat connection. At least you can cool yourself in the stream, and the shade from the towering cliffs provides some respite from the sun when it's not directly overhead.

Generally the best walking months are January and February — perhaps April, if it's not too wet, May and early June, September (likewise, if it's not too wet!), October, November and December. All lovers of mountainous islands, and certainly all walkers, will know that these rough guidelines are rules to which every year proves to be an exception — and freak weather, with heavy snow on the *sierra*, is not unknown in May!

A full weather report always appears, complete with meteorological maps, in the daily newspapers and on television every evening following the main news. For more information, you can telephone the 'Información Meteorológica' (Tel: 094) at any time of the day or night; be warned: the recorded message is in Spanish. Perhaps you can ask your hotel porter to interpret for you!

Always take a sunhat with you, even in mild weather; the sun is hotter than you think, in spite of the pleasantly cool sea breezes.

What to take

If you're already on Mallorca when you find this book, and haven't any special equipment such as a rucksack, boots or a torch, you can still make some of the walks — or buy yourself some equipment at any of the sports shops in Palma. Don't attempt the more difficult walks without the proper equipment. For each walk in the book, the *minimum* equipment is listed. Where walking boots are required, there is, unfortunately, no substitute: you will need to rely on the grip and ankle support they provide, as well as their waterproof qualities. All other walks should be made with stout shoes, preferably with thick rubber soles, to grip on wet or slippery surfaces.

You may find the following checklist useful:

walking boots (which *must* be broken in and comfortable)
up-to-date transport timetables from the Tourist Office (see page 9)
waterproof rain gear (outside summer months)
plastic bottle and water purifying tablets
long-sleeved shirt for sun protection
long trousers, tight at the ankles
bandages and band-aids
protective sun cream
plastic plates, cups etc
knives and openers
anorak (zip opening)
2 light cardigans
map (see page 59)
extra pair of socks
spare bootlaces
plastic groundsheet
plastic rain hat
sunhat
torch
whistle
compass
insect repellant
small rucksack

Please bear in mind that I've not made every walk in this book under *all* weather conditions, and I may not realise just how hot — or wet — some walks might be. The sun may be your worst enemy. It's tempting to walk in shorts and to forget that, with the sun behind you, the backs of your neck and legs are being badly burned. *Always* carry a long-sleeved shirt and long trousers to put on when you've had enough sun, and *always* wear a sunhat on bright days. It's a good idea as well to cover yourself generously with a protective sun cream. In hot weather, take your lunch in a shaded spot. Your good judgement will help you to modify the equipment list according to the season.

Responsibilities of the walker — a country code

The experienced ramber is used to following a 'country code' on his walks, but the tourist out for a lark may unwittingly cause damage, harm animals, and even endanger his own life. A code for behaviour is important wherever people roam over the countryside, but especially so on Mallorca — where you often cross private land, and where the rugged terrain can lead to dangerous mistakes.

- **Only light fires** at picnic areas with fireplaces. Stub cigarettes out with care.

- **Do not frighten animals.** The goats and sheep you may encounter on your walks are not tame. By making loud noises or trying to touch or photograph them, you may cause them to run in fear and be hurt.

- **Walk quietly through all farms** and take care not to provoke the dogs. Ignore their barking and keep your walking stick out of their sight — remember, it is only to be shown to an unfriendly, *unchained* dog.

- **Leave all gates just as you found them,** whether they are at farms or on the mountainside. Although you may not see any animals, the gates *do* have a purpose — generally to keep goats or sheep in — or out of — an area. Here again, animals could be endangered by careless behaviour.

- **Protect all wild and cultivated plants.** Don't try to pick wild flowers or uproot saplings. They will die before you even get back to your hotel. Obviously fruit and other crops are someone's private property and should not be touched. **Never** walk over cultivated land.

- **Take all your litter back to the hotel with you.**

- **DO NOT TAKE RISKS!** This is the most important point of all. Do not attempt walks beyond your capacity, and do not wander off the paths described if there is any sign of mist or if it is late in the day. **Do not walk alone,** and **always** tell a responsible person — perhaps your hotel porter — *exactly* where you are going and what time you plan to return. Remember, if you become lost or injure yourself, it may be a long time before you are found. On any but a very short walk near to villages, be sure to take a compass, whistle, torch, extra water and warm clothing — as well as some high-energy food, like chocolate.

3

4

6
8

5

7
9

10

11
12

Organisation of the walks

The twenty-five rambles in the book are grouped in three general areas. Walks 1—7 are easily reached from Palma, by public transport, in an hour or less. Walks 8—16 radiate from the northern mountain route, the C710 (see **STOP PRESS**, page 168). Walks 17—25 are centred on the Pollensa—Artá axis and the bays of Pollensa and Alcudia.

I hope that the book is set out so that you can plan your walks easily — depending on how far you want to go, your abilities and equipment, and the season.

You might begin by considering the large colour fold-out map between pages 20 and 21. Here you can see at a glance the overall terrain, the road network, and the exact orientation of the walking maps in the text. On the back of the map, you'll also find a key to the photographs — there's at least one for each walk, to give you an idea of the landscape.

Having selected one or two potential excursions from the map and the photographs, turn to the relevant walk. At the top of the page you'll find planning information: distance/hours, grade, equipment, and how to get there by public transport. If the grade and equipment specifications are beyond your scope, don't despair! *There's always at least one short version of each walk*, and in most cases these are far less demanding of agility and equipment!

When you are on your walk, you will find that the text begins with an introduction to the overall landscape and then quickly turns to a detailed description of the route itself. The large-scale maps (generally 1:40,000) have been specially annotated and set out facing the walking notes wherever possible. Times are given for reaching certain key checkpoints. Giving times is always tricky, because they depend on so many factors, but the times given fall in the range 2.4—3km per hour, depending on the terrain. Note that these times **include only minimal stops** — to catch your breath or take a photo. Be sure to allow extra time for other breaks — picnicking, swimming, sunbathing.

Many of the symbols used on the walking maps are self-explanatory, but here is a key to the most important ones:

▬ corresponds to red roads on the colour map	ᨒᨒ *canaleta* (p154)	▣ *atalaya* (p153)
══ corresponds to white roads on the colour map	∘∘∘ tunnel	♦/♣ monastery/*ermita*
═══ track or trail	▬▬ long walk	♣ church or chapel
--- path or steps	📷 best views	▯/◪ castle/in ruins
+++ railway	620 height (m)	A reference points for short and
	♦ danger— vertigo	B alternative walks
	Ⓖ guide (p58)	Ⓟ picnics (see p12)

1 SAN TELMO · CA'N TOMEVI · LA TRAPA · LA TORRE DE CALA BASET · SAN TELMO

Distance: 8km/4¾mi; about 3h

Grade: fairly easy, but it is an uphill climb most of the way to La Trapa, with some scrambling over rocks; path undefined at times

Equipment: walking boots, anorak, sunhat, picnic, water, torch

How to get there: 🚌 to Andraitx, but see NB below
Depart Palma 07.10 and every 45 minutes thereafter until 19.30; arrive Andraitx one hour later
Taxi from Andraitx to San Telmo
To return: taxi from San Telmo to Andraitx
🚌 from Andraitx to Palma
Departs Andraitx every 45min from 07.30 to 19.30; journey time 1h
NB: On Sundays *only*, there is a bus from Palma direct to San Telmo and return; dep Palma 09.00; dep San Telmo 17.15; journey time 1½h

Short walk: A→B→C→A takes in some highlights and avoids the climb to La Trapa: 3.5km/2mi; 1¼h. Follow the main walk, but at Ca'n Tomeví, turn left by a pine tree, *before* the path to La Trapa. From here, follow the notes in the last three paragraphs on page 72

A bout seven kilometres along the winding country road from Andraitx, the peaceful and picturesque summer resort of San Telmo reclines on the south coast, looking out across the stretch of deep blue waters towards the rocky island of Sa Dragonera. There are many pretty woodland walks in this area, but by far the most interesting is a visit to the ruins of the ancient Trappist monastery, some 380m/ 1250ft up on the rocky cliffside, facing out towards the distant Spanish mainland. This low stretch of pine-covered coastline is also the home of a variety of birds, including red kites, rock sparrows, and alpine swifts.

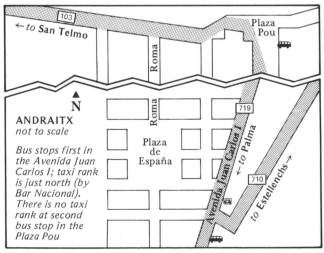

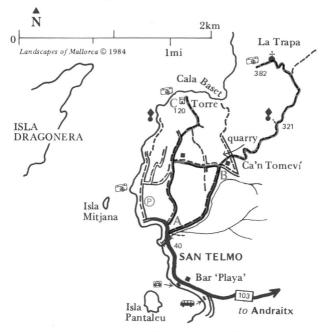

Any season permits a walk on this headland, but avoid the climb to La Trapa in summer. On cool days, remember to take warm clothing: the fresh winds coming off the sea can make it very chilly up at the monastery ruins.

From the bus stop in San Telmo, continue west along the coast road (PM103), crossing the bridge. Find the wide track track off right, just *before* the sign 'Vista Dragonera' (this is just 800m beyond the bus stop). **Start the walk** by turning right on this track; a dry-stone wall runs along at the right, with a windmill just behind it. Stay on this main track, ignoring the smaller offshoot to the right, and you'll come to Ca'n Tomeví in **15min**. There's an old winehouse here, where you can fortify yourself before the climb to come!

From Ca'n Tomeví take the path straight ahead, following the red arrow painted on a pine tree by a clearing. Pass a sandstone quarry on your left, and start to climb. Cross a track (a left turn here leads to the pretty cove of Cala Baset) and continue straight on, beside a barbed-wire fence. There is a red 'T' painted on a tree. From here on the path is sometimes hard to distinguish. Climb up, rounding the headland, with good views of Sa Dragonera and Sa Pantaleu, a large rock jutting up out of the sea. Higher up, where the trees have thinned out, you'll have to scramble over some rocks, and when you reach what seems to be the top of the cliff, keep a very sharp watch for the red arrows that point to the right, where the path climbs over some large rocks and boulders. If you miss this, you will come to a rather precipitous edge. Once over the brow of the cliff, you will be able to see the ruins of the monastery ahead. The going is a lot easier now: the path runs alongside the coastline, through more pines, and descends gently. About 150m (yds) before La Trapa, you'll see a path leading off to the right, which crosses the mountains to join the coastal C710; keep left, and reach La Trapa at about **1h10min**.

La Trapa is set back from the cliff edge on a series of grassy, sloping terraces, right by the side of an enormous *ombu* tree. Trappist monks lived here until the end of the eighteenth century, when the Spanish government abolished many of these institutions for both political and financial reasons. Recently, it has come under the protection of the Balearic Ornithological Group, who hope to keep this land safe from the ever-encroaching tentacles of *la urbanización*. Walk on round, past the monastery and the lovely almond tree-planted terrace, where the remains of an old mill face across to the ruins. If you continue on to the *mirador*, be careful of the steep drops to the sea. Back past the old mill, you can explore the neat stone steps that lead from one terrace to another and find the old well, or fountain, hiding at the end of a tunnel — if you brought a torch. There are several good spots for picnicking — including inside the ruins, should you get caught in a shower!

The way back is by the same route, until you re-reach Ca'n Tomeví (**2h**). Here turn right at the pine tree by the open clearing and follow the sandy track. Keep left five minutes on, going alongside a wire fence, following the red daubs on the trees. Meet another track crossing at right angles, but keep straight on and climb steadily, with good views of San Telmo's bay. Soon the track ends, but we follow the small path ahead, passing a ruined stone hut, and a minute later come out onto a wide track. Here turn up right. Five minutes later, the wide track ends; follow the red arrow pointing right along the main trail through the trees. Pass through two small clearings and, keeping left, arrive at the Torre de Cala Baset (**2h30min**).

You can climb the iron rungs to the lookout on top, from where you will see the rocky cove of Cala Baset below on your right and, to the left, over the water, Sa Dragonera, with its own *atalaya* on the top-most point of the island.

Go back along the same route, this time simply following the wide main track, which leads back to San Telmo (**3h**).

Distance: 9km/5½mi; 3½h

Grade: not difficult, but there is a climb of 350m/1200ft

Equipment: stout shoes, sunhat, cardigan, picnic, water

How to get there: 🚌 to Esporles (journey time 30min)
Summer: dep 10.00; *winter:* dep 12.00 Mo–Fri, 09.00 Sat, 10.00 Sun
To return: 🚌 from Esporles to Palma (journey time 30min)
Summer: dep 15.30; *winter:* dep 18.40 (weekdays), 15.00 (Sat–Sun)

Short walk (only possible if you have a car): from Son Ferrá to the *mirador* (A→B→A: 3km/1¾mi; 1¼h *return*); a climb of 200m/650ft. Equipment as above. Park well 'tucked in' by the Son Ferrá gates

Amidst undulating hills and valleys, where olive trees, almonds and carobs abound, a small country lane winds its way up from the centre of Esporles towards the *finca* of Son Ferrá, from where an old footpath climbs the wooded slopes of Na Boscana up to a *mirador* and an *ermita*.

The walk begins at the signpost to 'Es Verger'. Follow the country lane gradually uphill for about **40min**, keeping a lookout for a wooden gate on your right, where the word 'Ermita' is painted in red on a stone wall. (The gate is about 50m (yds) below the gates to Son Ferrá, so even if you miss it, you can quickly return.)

Join the wide path behind the gate to start the fairly steep climb. In **1h25min** you'll reach a small clearing, where a yellow signpost shows the way to 'Monumento' up right — the *mirador* and its monument to Christ — a ten-minute walk from here. Cross a *sitja* and soon come to the viewpoint, from where the panorama will hold you enthralled. Esporles lies below in the valley, between pine-covered hills, with the higher mountains of the Sierra de Tramuntana behind, and the rolling countryside sweeping down to where the city of Palma cradles the wide blue bay.

From here it's a climb of 15 minutes more, should you wish to visit the (closed) *ermita*, before you make your leisurely descent back to Esporles. If you have time, the northern entrance to the village is exceptionally pretty, and you might like to visit the thirteenth-century church.

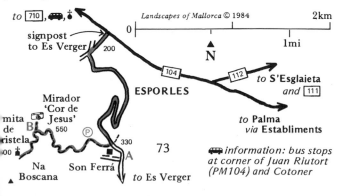

3 BUNYOLA · MIRADOR LEANDRO XIMENIS

Distance: 9km/5½mi; about 3¾h
Grade: not difficult, but there is a climb of about 400m/1300ft
Equipment: stout shoes, sunhat, cardigan, picnic, water
How to get there: Soller 🚂 to Bunyola (or bus: see page 159)
Depart Palma 08.00, 10.40, 13.00, 15.15; arr Bunyola 20min later
To return: 🚂 from Bunyola to Palma
Departures at 12.15, 14.35, 18.45; journey time 20min
Short walk: as far as you like along the path of the main walk; A→B
takes under 1¼h return and affords good views with little climbing

Olive trees and terraces, with sweeping views of the *sierras* are an early reward on this walk, easily reached from Bunyola station. **Start out** by turning left down the country road, to join the main C711. Here turn right, pass by the restaurant 'Ca'n Penaso' and continue for 800m (yds), to find the sign to 'Alquería d'Avall' on the left (**30min**), where the route to a *mirador* atop the Alquería peak begins.

Turn up left to the farmhouse, taking the first left just before the buildings, and going through the black iron gates. The guard dog here is extremely menacing, and his chain is long; you can squeeze by just to the left of him. If you carry a stout stick (keep it at your side — do *not* threaten him), he will stay well clear of you. After you've gone through two more sets of gates, you'll find a lovely picnic spot, on the first S-bend, overlooking olive groves — just out of view of the farmhouse. Then enjoy good views of Bunyola, before the track plunges deep into woodlands.

Still keeping to the main track, zig-zag up the shaded mountainside, passing some old wells and shelters, until at about **1h40min** you reach a level area. Here, as the track bends to the left through trees, find the worn stone steps to the *mirador*. Twenty minutes more, along a narrow, climbing path will bring you to the viewpoint, where you'll find splendid vistas, an old shelter, a well and a fireplace. Allow over an hour and a half for the return to Bunyola's station.

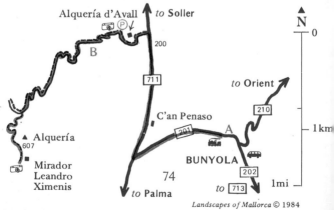

Landscapes of Mallorca © 1984

4 SANTA EUGENIA · SES COVES · PUIG D'EN MARRON · SANTA EUGENIA

Distance: 7.5km/4½mi; under 2¾h

Grade: easy — moderate ascents

Equipment: stout shoes, sunhat, picnic, water, mosquito repellant

How to get there: 🚌 to Santa Eugenia; ask for 'Ses Coves'
Depart Palma 13.30 Mon—Sat, 9.00 Sundays; arrive 35min later
To return: 🚌 from Santa Eugenia (outside the school) to Palma
Departs 15.15; arrives Palma 15.45; departs 18.00 Sundays/holidays

Short walk: A→B→C (Plaza España to cross monument, down through pass between boulders (see p77, second paragraph), turn left at foot of the hill, and return to Santa Eugenia by the Camino de las Ollerías: 2.5km/1½mi; under 1h); easy climb of 100m/325ft

Enjoy this delightful country walk at any time of year. The Puig d'en Marron is covered in pines, and the caves hiding in the hillsides contain silent memories of the past.

Having asked the bus driver for 'Ses Coves', **begin the walk** by following the narrow country lane up right into the rocky hills. (If you come by car, leave it in Santa Eugenia and walk to this lane — 15min northwest of the village on the main road (PM104); the lane is then on your *left*.)

In **20min** you'll come to a bend in the road, where an old abandoned stone well sits. Be sure not to take the track leading off to the right here, but continue on up the road, passing by the gnarled and ancient olive tree. Now the old stone houses of Ses Coves (the caves) gradually come into view, silently looking out over the plain through a maze of pricky-pear cacti. Soon you'll catch your first view of the caves themselves. In the biggest of these is an old wine-press. This ancient-looking object was last used in the early 1920s, and behind the mysterious wooden door, half hidden by the undergrowth, are the dark, cool wine cellars, where the enormous vats are still stored away, forgotten. The hills here are riddled with many other caves, where pirates used to store their smuggled goods, and which were also used as dwelling-places by the Moors hundreds of years ago.

At **25min** the road divides into two, left and right. Take the turning to the left, which leads you around the foot of the Puig d'en Marron, past some modern weekend chalets taking refuge in this sheltered little valley. On your left-hand side there's an unfinished cross monument.

At **30min** wide iron gates confront you. This is the entrance to the *puig*. Once through the gates, your uphill climb begins. In spring, the beautiful song of the nightingale is the only sound that echoes in the pine-scented silence. You will see hoopoes, and wild rabbits scurrying into the undergrowth, as your footsteps disturb their peace. Some excellent views of the plain below are to be had at various points, especially on the sharp bend further up.

At **50min** the road ends, dividing into two tracks. It is not possible to get lost on this small mountain, if you always keep to the right along the main track. (The track straight ahead takes you through tall pines to the south side of the mountain, with some superb views of the southeast part of the island and the distant airport with its ribbon-like runways. It is also possible to descend the mountain here by turning left onto the Camino de las Ollerías and following down into Santa Eugenia.)

But we turn right; the trees thin out in about 15 minutes, giving way to a large open space which covers the brow of the mountain. Up here, a good deal of the island may be seen. Turn left, following alongside the line of trees, in the direction of a square stone monument: now the magnificent mountain range stretches out before you along the west coast, with Es Pla (the plain) immediately before you. The town of Inca and Palma city are visible, as well as so many other towns and hamlets dotting the landscape. Explore this open tableland to find the best vantage points, and then find a good spot to picnic — you'll be an item of some interest to the inquisitive mountain goats wandering about!

To start down the mountain, follow the same route until you reach the gates guarding the *puig*. Once in the valley again, turn right, in the opposite direction from which you came, following the tarmac path. Pass by the ancient Arab burial ground, set back on the slopes at the left. While to the casual observer it is simply a mound of rocks and boulders, covered with pricky-pear cactus, excavations here in the early 1900s revealed human bones and relics dating back to the eighth and tenth centuries, when the Moors invaded and settled on the island.

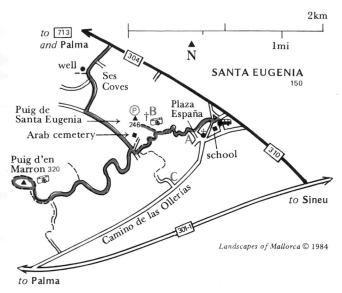

Landscapes of Mallorca © 1984

About 150m (yds) past the burial grounds, ignoring the first left-hand cart track, take the sandy cart track to the left. Pass a gated, arched entrance to an old well and take the first left turn past the well, on a sandy track, heading for the cross monument. This track ends at a chalet. At its right, find the gap in the stone wall (marked with a vertical red paint daub) and climb an easily-seen footpath. As you climb, the cross monument will be on your left and a strange-looking 'UFO'-type object on your right. It's really an old seacraft converted into a weekend hideaway!

We soon approach a pass: just before it, there's a natural rocky platform between two boulders. This is a good place to admire the view — good also for picnicking, because it's protected from the winds that harrass the plain. As soon as you clamber up between the boulders, the winds which usually blow straight across the plain will catch at your clothing and sting your cheeks. This is an exhilarating moment, as you look down on Es Pla, with the tang of the sea blowing on the wind. Now climb over the stone wall at the left, and make for the cross monument, from where almost all of the island is visible. Back down on the main path, turn left past a large, knarled pine, through low scrub, until at **2h30min** you come to a rough, walled-in, stony track, barred by a locked gate. There is a gap in the wall, through which you can scramble, to continue on down to Santa Eugenia, easily seen and just ten minutes from here.

5 VALLDEMOSSA · MIRADOR DE SES PUNTES · CAMINO DEL ARCHIDUQUE · EL TEIX

Distance: 14km/8½mi; 6½h

Grade: strenuous. **G** beyond the Mirador de Ses Puntes, where the paths are not always easy to find, there is a possibility of sudden thick mists, and a **danger of vertigo**

Equipment: walking boots, long trousers, picnic, water, whistle, cardigans, compass; in winter anorak, hat, gloves, extra rations

How to get there: 🚌 to Valldemossa
Depart Palma 10.00; arrive Valldemossa 10.30 *winter*; in *summer* there is an earlier departure at 07.45; arrives Valldemossa 08.15
To return: 🚌 from Valldemossa to Palma
Departs 16.00, 18.30 *winter*; departs 15.30, 17.00, 19.30 *summer*; journey time ½h

Short walks: no guide required for either; both are strenuous, Short walk 1 the more so; picnic, water, sunhat, extra clothing in winter

1 Valldemossa to the Mirador de Ses Puntes and return (A→B→A: 6km/3¾mi; 2½h); follow course of main walk and return same way

2 Valldemossa to ICONA shelter below El Teix (A→C→A: 6km/3¾mi; 2½h); go right on road *in front of* Son Gual; when it turns off right in a hairpin bend, fork left up track; stout shoes will suffice

Alternative walk: Combine Short walk 2 with the scramble to the summit of El Teix (add 1½h; boots essential; **G**)

O ne of the island's best walks, boasting splendid views *and* much historical interest. Moreover, it offers so many permutations that any walker with energy can tackle a suitable *part* of the walk, depending on the season. The main route follows a trail up into the thickly-wooded mountains near Valldemossa, joins the Camino del Archiduque, rounds the edge of the high plateau with its fantastic coastal views (and exciting sheer drops!), climbs and scrambles up to the summit of El Teix, and then drops back down to Valldemossa through the pretty Cairats valley. ICONA have recently taken over the Cairats valley area, making the downward trek much easier along an ample (but somewhat steep) track, dotted with various points of interest: you'll find examples of the charcoal industry, thrush-netting, burnt lime ovens, and a 'snow house' along the route, all signposted (see pages 12, 153-156).

The walk starts at the bus stop in Valldemossa, one of the island's tourist attractions, described on page 24. From the *parada* walk back up the main (Palma) road (the way the bus has just come). You'll soon spot a very large old house with a tower — Son Gual — on the left. Turn left up the road before the house, and then take your first right. Left again before the house (unless you are making the Alternative walk — in which case continue on *past* Son Gual). Now continue straight uphill, through this new housing estate, until you come to the top of the hill, by a lovely stone wall. Here there is a sign on a lamppost, referring to various landmarks on our route. Turn left, then curve right round a large house. Here turn left up a track and follow it towards the beautiful group of umbrella pines. Just before you reach the pines, turn left up a stony path (**20min**), marked with a red paint daub.

Soon reach an old broken gate which you must climb; then continue ahead for about five minutes more, until you see the red arrow painted on a rock at a bend, which shows that our way now follows a rocky woodcutters' trail up to the right. Pass a *sitja* on the left (**40min**); just past here fork right and right again a few minutes later. In **50min** come to a 'cross-roads': go straight ahead to pass an old stone oven on the left. You'll soon meet a stone wall, where, again, you will have to climb over a gate (**1h**). Just beyond you'll reach level ground — an extensive and shaded open area — a good spot to take a quick rest. In this clearing, you'll see tracks left and right. But go straight ahead to find two forks out of the clearing: opt for the left hand one, and cross over a *sitja*. In **1h5min** you'll pass the well of Es Pouet (the water is *not* fit to drink). Soon the path begins to climb again, with the high, pine- and oak-wooded rocky mountain of Veyá on your right. At about **1h15min** you'll pass another *sitja*, and, just beyond it, another old stone oven hidden in the trees to the right.

Soon you glimpse the sea, and, forking left towards the *mirador*, there are excellent views of the coast. It's ten minutes more to the Mirador de Ses Puntes, from where you can see down the western coastline almost as far as Bañalbufar — if swirling mists don't play tricks on you!

Turn right from the *mirador* to follow the famous Camino del Archiduque, a stone-laid trail which climbs the Veyá mountain, dips into the valley of S'Estret de Son Gallart, and then climbs again onto the high plateau. The Archduke Luis Salvador (see also page 25), was very fond of walking and fell in love with Mallorca. Luckily for us, he possessed sufficient riches to build these mountain 'highways' for his walking pleasure.

About twenty minutes along from the *mirador*, take the path to the left, following the (infrequent) splashes of red paint. At **1h45min** climb a rocky slope to a geographical stone. As you continue straight ahead through the woods, notice how the branches of the trees are covered with a thick, lichen-type green moss, due to the humidity of the frequent mists that swirl around the mountaintops.

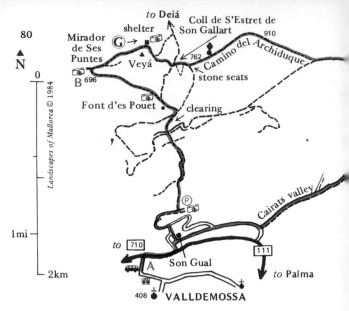

At **1h55min** climb up to an abandoned stone shelter, from where there are more magnificent views. Go straight down the opposite side of the shelter, keeping a sharp look-out for the small rock-piles and *very* sparse red paint daubs. At **2h5min** take the fork to the right; the left-hand turning leads to Deiá. Ten minutes later, you will arrive at a 'crossroads' in the valley called the Coll de S'Estret de Son Gallart. The path down right leads back to Es Pouet and the one left also to Deiá. Our *camino* continues ahead. Standing on the rocks here, you can see the distant Bay of Soller and the pretty mountain village of Deiá (see also page 26). Notice as well the strange tree formations down the immediate slopes — deliberately cultivated this way for thrush-netting.

Now continue ahead, pass a gap in the old stone wall and come to a rest area with stone seats. From here, an easily-followed path leads right down to Es Pouet. Our way passes to the left of the seats and begins its steep 20-minute climb to the high plateau. Once up on the *meseta*, you can see forever! There are splendid views on all sides. Right down the coastline, Galatzó pushes its peak through the scudding clouds. Deiá lies hundreds of feet below — also the famous Foradada (the rock pierced with a hole), that juts out into the sea near Son Marroig. The Bay of Soller reposes peacefully under the Mediterranean sun, and to the south, Palma's bay glistens like a huge round mirror, with the high cliffs of Cabo Blanco on the horizon. But this path skirts the edge of the plateau, with very precipitous drops to the left: go with a guide and be *extra* vigilant along here if it's misty!

Teix
1063

ont
d'es
Polls

ICONA
C shelter

Es Caragol

G

At about **3h** into the walk, the Camino del Archiduque disappears, but there still exists a path of sorts continuing over the strewn rocks. Five minutes later, just by a small group of pines, a pile of rocks on the right indicates another way back to Es Pouet. Continue on towards the sparsely-grouped trees ahead, where you might stop and picnic in the company of sheep and rosemary-scented air. When you renew your journey along the rocky path, the peak of El Teix soon beckons (at **3h45min**). It looks deceivingly near, but it will take us about an hour and a half to scramble up to the top and return. There's no particular path, but it's a fairly easy climb for *experienced* mountain walkers. And the rewards are never-to-be-forgotten views of almost the entire island from the Teix summit at 1063m/ 3500ft!

Returning from El Teix, rejoin the rocky path which begins its descent into the Cairats valley. Soon you'll come to a *casa de nieve*, a large deep hole for storing snow (see pages 153-156).

At about **5h30min** walking, having met a new, wider track, you will arrive at the very pleasant new ICONA shelter. Complete with a large fireplace, wooden tables and benches, it is an ideal place to shelter, rest, or enjoy a tasty meal roasted over a wood fire.

Continue on down the steep winding track, to pass the Font d'es Polls (the Poplars' Well) some eight minutes later. The large poplar trees growing here have lent their name to this ancient well. If you're making Short walk 2 or the Alternative walk, you may wish to tackle the steep path here, leading up the cliffside of Es Caragol.

It's not too long before you see a new ICONA signpost indicating the way to the Industria del Carbón, and further down the ever-descending track, you'll pass by an old *horno de calç* in ruins and one or two more *sitjas*, before coming to a second signpost to a typical burnt lime oven. A few minutes later, you can visit the 'Coll de Caçar', also signposted (see pages 153-156).

After **6h** walking come to a large gate in a stone wall and meet a second gate ten minutes on; soon the track ends and you find a curving tarmac road (part of the new housing estate). Fork right here, and follow the road to the front of Son Gual. You'll reach the big house in **6h30min** walking.

6 PUERTO DE SOLLER · S'ILLETA

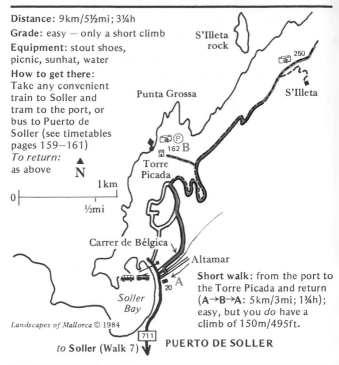

Distance: 9km/5½mi; 3¼h

Grade: easy — only a short climb

Equipment: stout shoes, picnic, sunhat, water

How to get there:
Take any convenient train to Soller and tram to the port, or bus to Puerto de Soller (see timetables pages 159–161)
To return:
as above

N

0 |————————| 1 km
          ½mi

Landscapes of Mallorca © 1984

S'Illeta rock

Punta Grossa

S'Illeta

Torre Picada

Carrer de Bélgica

Altamar

Soller Bay

Short walk: from the port to the Torre Picada and return (A→B→A: 5km/3mi; 1¾h); easy, but you *do* have a climb of 150m/495ft.

to **Soller** (Walk 7)   **PUERTO DE SOLLER**

L a Torre Picada, a seventeenth-century watchtower atop the hill called Sa Punta Grossa, commands very fine views of Puerto de Soller and the surrounding rocky coast. For further adventure, you can follow the trail along the coast as far as S'Illeta and admire the wild and rugged panorama of rocky mountains and deep blue sea.

Start out at the Altamar snack bar, south of the tram/bus stops. Turn uphill, and then cross the streambed by going left over the bridge. Now turn right: this road becomes the Carrer de Bélgica and climbs up through a housing estate. When it divides in two (**25min**), turn up right by the block of flats. After about 100m (yds), the road ends at a gate. Pass through the access gate on the right and follow the stony track until at **45min**, you come to a fork; from here it's five minutes up left to the *atalaya*. The tower is closed to prevent further damage by vandals, but there are excellent views all round. The rocky islet of S'Illeta is visible to the north, and the small headland of Ses Puntes below.

Back at the fork, continue along the coast until the path ends opposite S'Illeta (**1h50min**). The wild landscape along here offers untold opportunities for keen photographers!

82

7 SOLLER · BINIARAIX · ES BARRANC · FINCA DE L'OFRE · ES CORNADORS · S'ARROM · SOLLER

Distance: 16km/9¾mi; 7h

Grade: strenuous, but along clearly defined paths most of the way. The ascent of 900m/2950ft is tiring

Equipment: stout walking shoes or boots, cardigan, anorak, sunhat, picnic, water purifying tablets (or water in summer months)

How to get there: 🚂 to Soller
Depart Palma 08.00; arrive Soller 09.00 (there is another departure at 10.40, but the train is usually very crowded, and you would not have enough time to complete the long walk)
To return: 🚂 from Soller to Palma
Departs Soller 14.10 and 18.20; arrives Palma one hour later (a later train departs Soller 21.00 Sundays and *fiesta* days only)

Short walk: Soller to Biniaraix (A→B) and on up the path of Es Barranc as far as you like for good views without too much climbing; it will take 1¼h from Soller to Biniaraix *and return*; equipment as above; boots not necessary

Alternative walk: Cuber reservoir to Soller (C→B→A; 12km/7¼mi; 4½h); easy, but steep descent to Biniaraix. See map notes page 85

T his is surely one of the most beautiful walks on the island! There are leafy glades, impressive cliff-sides, waterfalls, green valleys, rocky mountains, and magnificent views from the Mirador de l'Ofre — at 955m/3135ft, it's certainly worth the effort it takes to get there! Be sure to check the weather forecast before making this walk; it would be a shame to get all the way up to the *mirador*, only to find the Soller valley covered in low-lying mists. The best time of year is on a clear, cool spring day.

The little old 'wild west'-type train whistles its way into the pretty village of Soller at about nine o'clock. You will have been enthralled by your scenic train journey out of Palma into the countryside and up into the foothills, through a long dark tunnel under the Sierra de Alfabia, and finally down from amazing heights right into this quaint station.

Follow the other passengers down the station steps, and continue on down the narrow street for a couple of minutes until you reach the Plaça de Sa Constitució (there is a map of Soller on page 88). Fill your water bottles from the fountain in the middle of the square, and then follow the signposts to Biniaraix and Fornalutx, pointing right down a long, narrow street. **Start the walk here,** and follow along this main thoroughfare for about fifteen minutes, until you reach the crossroads, where a second signpost to Biniaraix pointing straight ahead indicates that you are on the right way. Continue along, crossing a small bridge over the Torrente d'es Barranc on the left, and following this

83

narrow lane uphill until you arrive at the picturesque little hamlet of Biniaraix at **35min**. You will find yourselves in the tiny village square, which is dominated by a large tree. On the right, above the Calle de S José, is a signpost 'Lluc a pie' (Lluc on foot); this is the route you will follow. A minute later, turn sharp right: you will see the footpath beginning straight ahead, signed 'Camí d'es Barranc'. On the left are the village washhouse and the filters which purify its water supply.

(There are also alternative routes to Fornalutx from here: the car route — signed 'Fornalutx 1km' — and the Camí d'es Marroigs. Don't be deceived: Fornalutx is over 2km north by the first route and 3km by the second; see map if you'd like to make one of these walks another day.)

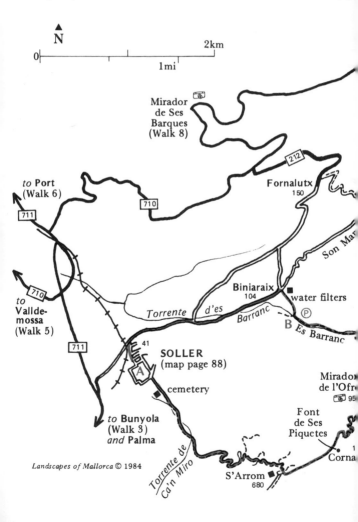

Landscapes of Mallorca © 1984

Following along on the main walk, begin your climb up Es Barranc. In a few minutes, pass a gate on the left with a 'no entry' sign on it. Our path continues along to the right, down the rough stony steps, following the red arrow and the words 'L'Ofre, Lluc a peu'.

At about **45min** cross a small bridge — the first past Biniaraix — over the stream, and continue on up the stony steps. These can be a bit slippery if it has been a frosty morning. The grassy terraced slopes, which were once cultivated right up the mountainside, are populated by centuries-old olive trees, mis-shapen into artistic forms of sculpture. The rushing waters of the stream echo mystically around you . . . certainly a magical place, especially early in the morning as the mists are rising!

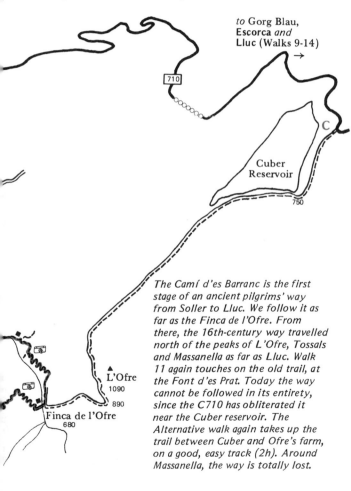

to Gorg Blau,
Escorca *and*
Lluc (Walks 9-14)
→

710

C

Cuber
Reservoir

750

*The Camí d'es Barranc is the first
stage of an ancient pilgrims' way
from Soller to Lluc. We follow it as
far as the Finca de l'Ofre. From
there, the 16th-century way travelled
north of the peaks of L'Ofre, Tossals
and Massanella as far as Lluc. Walk
11 again touches on the old trail, at
the Font d'es Prat. Today the way
cannot be followed in its entirety,
since the C710 has obliterated it
near the Cuber reservoir. The
Alternative walk again takes up the
trail between Cuber and Ofre's farm,
on a good, easy track (2h). Around
Massanella, the way is totally lost.*

L'Ofre
1090

890

Finca de l'Ofre
680

At **55min** follow the main path, ignoring the small stone steps that lead up to the right. Just past here, a rather impressive cliff-face looms up before you on the right. Soon cross a second bridge over this curious stream which rushes along quite noisily and then disappears underground, so that one moment you can hear the water cascading over the rocks, and then all of a sudden you notice how silent it is!

An old stone house, once used by the olive-pickers, appears just up ahead at **1h20min**, where the path turns to the left. The remains of a small, tiled kitchen, with its fire place and chimney are still to be seen; you can easily imagine the old Mallorcan farmers — their faces gnarled as the ancient olive trees — sitting round chatting idly after a long day's olive-gathering.

At **1h45min** cross your third bridge, and soon a fourth and last bridge. A little further along, a fairly big house appears on the left, with a very neat stone wall surrounding it. Continue straight ahead here: you will see the word 'Lluc' painted in faded blue on the wall — also a big red arrow. (The path leading off to the left only goes to an ancient well in the mountains called Font d'es Verger.) Keep always to the main path, as one or two smaller ones appear on the right. At **2h** the main path takes a sharp turn to the left: be careful not to follow the flat earth path that leads on straight ahead of you.

It's a good idea to stop now and then from here on, not only to catch your breath, but to admire the scintillating views. The village of Soller seems so far away now, and the lighthouse in the Bay of Soller can also be seen. The cluster of houses at Biniaraix seems infinitely tiny — almost unreal.

As you proceed another fantastic cliff-face confronts you, full of holes in the rocks where falcons, wild pigeons and other birds have made their nests. A truly impressive waterfall cascades down this steep rock face after a heavy rainy season. Soon, a rugged deep ravine appears on the right, where the fury of the rushing waters echoes from far below. Just past here, you will come across the iron gates that guard the Finca de l'Ofre (**2h30min**). Don't be put off by the various signs — this is a public pathway, and you are quite at liberty to go through. Don't worry about the loose bulls wandering about here either; they're meek as lambs and terrified of humans! Painted on the brick walls of the farm building are clear indications of our route.

Our track is the one that leads off to the right, through the farm. Cross the flat area beyond a second, smaller farmhouse, to find the rocky mountain path to the Mirador de l'Ofre — which, confusingly enough, is on the Cornadors mountain! — straight ahead. (The peak of L'Ofre itself, on the trail to Lluc, soars up behind us at 1090m/3575ft.)

After 100m (yds), go through an old and rusty gate, where there is a rough sheep-hold just beyond on the right. Take a breather now, and turn to admire the high, silent Sierra of Alfabia on the left, together with the pretty valley and farmhouses below — a wonderful panorama.

Continue the stony ascent. If it's sunny, please wear a sunhat — there's no shade to be found until you reach the shelter at the top, and the sun is now quite high. You will pass by two unusual stone columns, formed by the wind, and climb a fence, aided by wooden hand-made ladders, until at **3h40min** you reach the point where the rocky pathway divides in two. Turning up to the right, the path leads you to the low stone shelter. Now, scramble across the rocks and boulders, over the brow of Es Cornadors, to find the fabulous *mirador*.

The views from here are truly breath-taking: the whole of the valley of Soller lies like a miniature toy world far below you, and the fairy-tale villages of Biniaraix and Fornalutx appear like small blotches on a neat, green copybook. Beyond lies the distant Bay of Soller and all round the magnificence of the mountains: the Sierra de Alfabia, the Coll de Soller, El Teix, the Puig Mayor, L'Ofre.

Return now, across the rocks and back to the shelter — a good place to have your picnic lunch. The shade offered by the stone building is quite welcome on a sunny day, and you can admire the views from the south side of Es Cornadors. After having your fill of food and views, return to where the rocky path divides into two, this time continuing on down to the right. At **4h** cross over the stone wall by means of the iron ladders that bypass the locked gate. Now you will find the path not nearly so rocky and uncomfortable, and the shade from the evergreens makes a welcome respite. Follow on, through these pleasantly cool, leafy glades, with nothing but the smell of pines and the distant chiming of the church bells of Soller to accompany you. At **4h30min** a small grassy *sitja* appears on the left, and five minutes further along, you'll pass by a rusty iron gate on the right, soon going through some broken old wooden gates. At **4h30min** small stone steps lead up left to an old spring, the Font de Ses Piquetes (best to use purifying tablets if you take on water here). The main path passes through another iron gate a few metres (yards) further along. About 100m (yds) past this gate, take a sharp turn to the right, where there is a small path leading downwards, just by the side of a large pine tree. The continuing path later doubles back to meet this narrower path further down, so there is no danger of getting lost! Continue on down the rough stone steps, and at the bottom turn right, past a big old farmhouse. Past the house, take the track to the left and continue through the farm of S'Arrom, passing through two sets of iron gates and following on down the wide, stony track. At about **5h10min**, just by a rough lean-to used as a car port, the way divides into two again. The left hand track through the gates just leads to the house; we go right and then swing round left through some gates behind the house. Five minutes later, take the turning to the left through more gates, where you will find the word 'Soller' painted in blue on the rocky wall. Continue now, an easy descent, along a wide, winding track. At **6h** a tall iron gate with spikes on top is usually locked, but you can pass through the small access gate on the right. Five minutes later, the track is surfaced for about 100m, just by a large house. Soon a small bridge crosses the Torrente de Ca'n Miro, and a few minutes later, a second bridge. Pass through yet another double iron gate. More and more little houses keep popping up as you draw nearer to Soller. Ignore the track off to the left and continue right, until at **6h30min** a wide bridge on your left crosses the stream, just by the side of an old stone *canaleta*. Turn right, down and away from the bridge, along the tarmac road and past the high-walled cemetery. Use the sketch map below to make your way to the station, where you will probably have time to sit with a drink in one of the bar-cafés, before boarding your train.

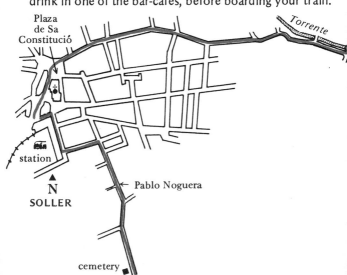

13
14

15

16

17

18

19

20

21

22

8 MIRADOR DE SES BARQUES · SA COSTERA · CALA TUENT · LA CALOBRA · SOLLER

Distance: 16km/9¾mi; 6h

Grade: moderate, with several ascents and descents (all on good tracks/trails)

Equipment: stout walking shoes (boots outside summer months), sunhat, insect repellant, cardigans and anorak in cold weather, picnic, plastic bottle with water purifying tablets (water in summer)

How to get there: 🚂 to Soller
Depart Palma 08.00; arrive Soller 09.00. *Taxi from Soller station to 'Mirador des Ses Barques';* but see also **STOP PRESS**, page 168
To return: 🚢 from La Calobra to Puerto de Soller (last departure 17.00; 🚌 from the port to Soller (dep 17.55) in time for the last 🚂 to Palma (dep 18.20 daily; a further departure 21.00 Sundays)
NB: The boat from La Calobra **only runs from May to September** and **will not take large groups.** If you are more than three or four, or if you make the walk outside summer, opt for the Alternative walk described below

Short walk: from the Mirador de Ses Barques as far as you like in the Bálitx valley, where you can picnic. Allow about one hour walking *return*, and be sure to ask the taxi driver to wait for you or to return for you (see p158); stout shoes, sunhat, picnic, water

Alternative walk: Mirador de Ses Barques to Sa Costera and return (A→B→A): 12km/7¼mi; under 5h); grade and equipment as main walk. Ask the taxi to return to the viewpoint for you (see p158)

T he Mirador de Ses Barques is one of the most scenic spots along this beautiful stretch of mountainous coastline near Soller. From over 400 metres we can take in the magnificent panorama of the village and its port in the valley below, surrounded by the high peaks of the *sierra* and the deep blue Mediterranean shimmering beneath in the sun. The *mirador* is also famous for its freshly squeezed orange juice, so why not enjoy a sparkling glassful of 'sunshine' before embarking on this hiking adventure?

The walk begins here at the viewpoint, just down on the right, past the piled-up crates of empty bottles, and through the open gates. The track is wide, flat and comfortable. Ignore all off-shoots and in **5min** you'll meet large green gates. Just past here, the artistically-cultivated terraced slopes, studded with a multitude of silvery-leaved olive trees, are especially picturesque. Soon you will be able to see the large old farmstead of Bálitx de Dalt (Bálitx on the Heights) ahead on the hillside. When the path forks at **15min**, go right through the rusty gates and enter the incredibly beautiful valley of Bálitx, where the footpath winds away over the hills into the distance, through myriad olive groves. Continuing on this main path, you'll see the remains of old *canaletas* below on the left.

At **20min** you'll see a stony path straight ahead. This

is a short cut worth taking, as it passes by the Font de Bálitx, a freshwater spring in a tunnel in the hillside. Outside summer months, you can take on water here. The short cut then rejoins the main track further down, just before the house of Bálitx d'en Midj, whereas the path leading from the spring up the hillside is an old route to Montcaire, unfortunately now closed to walkers..

Pass by the old abandoned farmhouse of Bálitx d'en Midj (Middle Balitx), with its large, splendid courtyard — now sadly in ruins. Sheep and pigs wander in and out in search of pastureland. Follow the track past the farm, and go through another rusty iron gate and

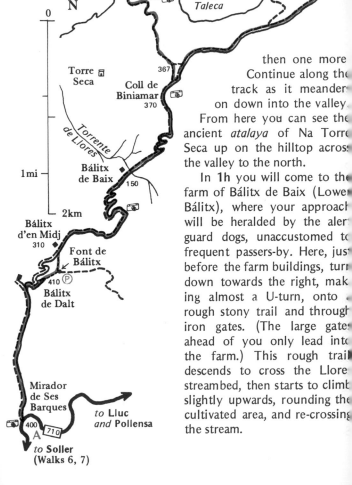

then one more Continue along the track as it meanders on down into the valley. From here you can see the ancient *atalaya* of Na Torre Seca up on the hilltop across the valley to the north.

In **1h** you will come to the farm of Bálitx de Baix (Lower Bálitx), where your approach will be heralded by the alert guard dogs, unaccustomed to frequent passers-by. Here, just before the farm buildings, turn down towards the right, making almost a U-turn, onto a rough stony trail and through iron gates. (The large gates ahead of you only lead into the farm.) This rough trail descends to cross the Lloret streambed, then starts to climb slightly upwards, rounding the cultivated area, and re-crossing the stream.

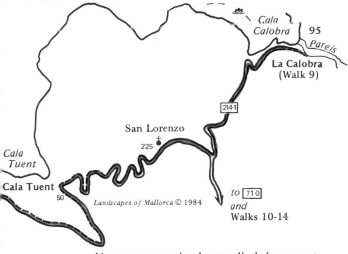

Now our route begins to climb in earnest, up to the Coll de Biniamar. This is a fairly steep ascent, taking about three-quarters of an hour. This climb can be quite unpleasant on a hot day: the valley traps all the sun's heat and not a breath of air moves to cool you. A sunhat is an absolute necessity during this climb! At about **1h50min** you will reach the *coll* where, thankfully, the path levels out a bit, before descending later towards the coast. Here, a cool and welcome breeze wafts through the trees.

Once on the heights, keep a sharp look-out for the path leading off down left to Sa Costera. You'll meet it in about five minutes' walking, just by a bend in the main track. A pile of rocks indicates the beginning of this narrow path, which starts by a type of gate entrance marked with red paint. Ignore the path on the right met in a few moments; it only rejoins the main Cala Tuent route. Continue down through the thickly pine-covered hillside towards the sea. It takes about half an hour to reach the cliffs at Sa Costera, where a large old house, mostly in ruins, overlooks the picturesque bay of Es Racó de Sa Taleca from its vantage point high up on the cliffs. Find the spring hiding in the dark stone tunnel, just up on a ridge behind the house, where you can cool your drinks in the icy water while you prepare your picnic lunch on the makeshift wooden table under the young olive tree. The blue waters of the bay below shimmer invitingly, and there is a (very steep) path down to the *cala*, but the energy required to venture down for a swim and then climb back up would far outweigh the pleasures of this excursion! Those making the Alternative walk will wend their way from here back to the Mirador de Ses Barques along the same route (under 5 hours).

Or, if you're lucky enough to be making the walk in the summer, let's carry on to Cala Tuent and La Calobra. You'll rejoin the main route in about **2h50min** walking. Turn left and wind your way on downhill, towards the ruins of an old electricity plant. You'll pass the small path leading down to it at about **3h15min** into the walk.

From here it's another hour and a quarter to the pretty little cove of Cala Tuent (**4h30min**). From Cala Tuent, follow the road (the first part of which is not asphalted) up and over the hill in the direction of La Calobra. This final ascent is rather irksome, but take a short break at the top to visit the small, thirteenth-century chapel of San Lorenzo, one of the oldest monuments on Mallorca, before you finally descend down into La Calobra (**6h**).

It's unlikely that you'll have any time to enjoy the hustle and bustle of this spot — perhaps the island's most-visited tourist attraction. But then, you may have more time for a relaxing drink and snack after you complete Walk 9! For today, give your feet a well-earned rest on the boat ride back to the Port of Soller, while you marvel at the high rocky cliffs reflected in the colourful waters, and at the rugged mountains behind, impressive and wild — adding beauty and colour to this truly spectacular landscape of Mallorca.

9 EL TORRENTE DE PAREIS

Distance: 7km/4¼mi; 4h from Escorca (10.5km/6¼mi; 6h *from Lluc*)

Grade: ⓖ; difficult. Rocks slippery and dangerous in places; only for experts

Equipment: walking boots, extra socks and cardigans, torch, whistle, sunhat, picnic, water, anorak in cool weather

How to get there: 🚌 to Inca (for Lluc); but see **STOP PRESS**, p168 Train departs Palma 09.00; arrives Inca 09.35; bus waits outside station and departs 09.45 for Lluc; arrives Lluc 10.20

To return: ⛴ from La Calobra: see notes Walk 8, page 93

Short walk: explore the gorge from La Calobra — an easy outing. Train to Soller; tram to the port; boat to La Calobra: find convenient times in the schedules p161. Sunhat, swimwear, picnic, wading shoes

---

Following the course of the Torrente de Pareis is perhaps the most spectacular excursion on foot in Mallorca. But it's not for the inexperienced: you'll have to scramble over slippery rocks and boulders, wade through pools — and maybe even swim! — if you make the walk early in summer, after a wet spring. And this *is* a walk for summer months only — May to September.

With luck, you'll find a taxi driver at Lluc, waiting for a client and willing to take you to Escorca; more likely, you'll have to take the route that starts at the left of the monastery and climbs past the Finca Son Massip (see map). The *times given below* are based on departure from the Restaurante de Escorca, where **the walk** really **begins**.

Opposite the restaurant at Escorca, go through the gates to the old thirteenth-century church of Sant Pere. Just past the church, take the steps on the left, up to the old olive tree, and follow the path to the right. Come to two gates, and go through the brown rusty gate on the left. When you come to a large waste-disposal bin, turn sharp left. Now follow down, alongside the low stone wall on the left and at **10min** climb over the small iron gate. Continue down the rocky path, and at **15min** be sure to *turn sharp left* at the olive tree with a black circle painted on it. Go down as far as the rocks, where you turn left again, and then right — red arrows now indicate the way, and the path also is easy to see from now on, as it winds on down towards the bed of the *torrente*. You can already see the gorge.

You'll reach the *voltes llargues* (the long bends) at **30min**, and in **1h** the path passes under the branches of a fig tree, where — some 20m (yds) or so further ahead, you must find the path off to the right, down through the rocks and long grasses. This is not easily seen, but starts more or less just as the main path begins to bend upwards again.

Five to ten minutes later should find you at the bottom,

97

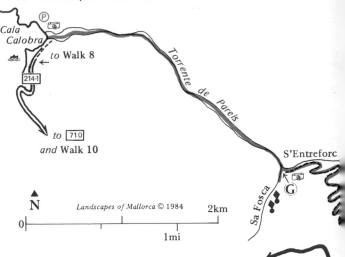

amongst the strewn rocks and
boulders of the Torrente de Lluc. The
scenery here is very impressive. Turn left
down the Torrente de Lluc and find the
small grassy path on the left that will lead you
first up above the rocks on the stream bed and then
down again into the wider Entreforc (**1h20min**). Here
at the Entreforc, the Torrente de Lluc unites with the
waters coming from Sa Fosca, to form the Torrente de
Pareis (the 'twin streams'). Down here, dwarfed by sheer
rock faces and vertical cliffs, the walker is surrounded by
a fantastic landscape. The strip of sky above seems far, far
away, and the cry of wild birds and the hollow bleat of
mountain goats echo mysteriously between the rock walls.

A large rock, more or less in the centre where the twin
torrents converge, has a red cross painted across the top,
showing Lluc to the south, La Calobra to the north, Sa
Fosca (the 'dark place') off to the left, and — written in
the Mallorcan dialect — 'Millor no enerí' (Better not go!),
indicating the sheer rock wall on the right.

Sa Fosca is a very exciting — and dangerous — place. It is
possible to venture a little way in, exploring up the slippery
high boulders. The walls of the gorge gradually close in
above, leaving you literally 'in the dark', and further in,
there are small underground lakes. *(Hardy and experienced
rock climbers, in guided groups, and equipped with ropes
and inflatable rafts, can penetrate the depths of Sa Fosca.
The first two explorers to do this, both Mallorcans, were
lost for forty-eight hours inside Sa Fosca — unable to find*

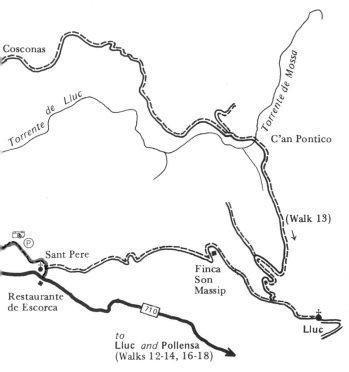

Cosconas

Torrente de Lluc

Torrente de Mossa

C'an Pontico

(Walk 13)

Sant Pere

Finca
Son
Massip

Restaurante
de Escorca

710

Lluc

to
Lluc *and* Pollensa
(Walks 12-14, 16-18)

their way out and unable to go back!) Be warned, if you decide to explore a bit in here, of a drop in temperature and of **the dangers involved.**

To begin down the Torrente de Pareis, follow over to the right from the red-painted rock, and find the small path that leads up through the long grass (there are one or two more red arrow guides).

And, really, from here on, explanations are superfluous. It is simply a matter of finding the best way down along the stream bed, over the rocks and through narrow passes between huge boulders. Occasional guide marks pop up, but there are not many of these. There are also several places where steeper drops have to be negotiated, but none of them are too difficult — although you may have to wet your feet. This is a very popular excursion with the Mallorcans, who regularly organise groups — sometimes of up to fifty people — and the easiest way to negotiate the difficult spots is to seek out the well-worn, bottom-polished rocks!

After about an hour and a quarter in the gorge, a small path leads off up to the left, rounding some impassable rocks — but this is well marked with arrows.

10 A RAMBLE ROUND THE PUIG MAYOR

Distance: 6 km/3¾mi; 2½h
Grade: easy after initial climb

Equipment: stout shoes, sunhat, plastic bottle with water purifying tablets (water in summer), anorak and cardigans in winter

How to get there: hired car (or taxi hired from Soller station) to K2.2 marker on the road to La Calobra; but see **STOP PRESS**, p168
To return: see 'Language hints', p157, if you wish to ask a taxi driver to return for you or to collect you on the C710

Short walk: as far as the oaks and return (A→B→A: 3km/1¾mi; 1h); equipment as above; easy after initial 15-20min climb

Alternative walk: via Coll d'es Carscolers to C710 (A→B→C→D: 5.5km/3¼mi; 2¼h); transport required on C710 — see map

T he deposits of a lagoon where, millions of years ago, prehistoric species abounded in the waters and swamps of the Eocene period, can still be found along a five or six kilometre band on the northern slopes of the Puig Mayor. This area, at a height of some 700—900m, runs from Es Clot near Fornalutx (Walk 7) as far as the fountain of Sa Baume, which we'll visit in this walk. Originally, the band was much longer and wider, but the violence with which the mountains thrust themselves upwards forced the strata up

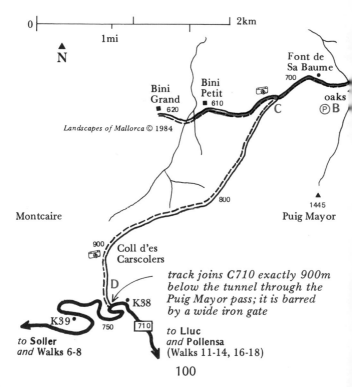

Landscapes of Mallorca © 1984

track joins C710 exactly 900m below the tunnel through the Puig Mayor pass; it is barred by a wide iron gate

to Soller and Walks 6-8

to Lluc and Pollensa (Walks 11-14, 16-18)

to their present height. The hard white rocks, originally fine mixtures of calcareous and lacustrine deposits, break off easily into thin slates of stone when hit, and these strata contain some of the richest fossil flora known on Mallorca. A walk along the northern slopes of the island's highest mountain gives us not only the chance to see some of these beautiful and interesting white rock formations, but also lets us admire the picturesque little valley of Bini, with its stream trickling down towards the cliffs, as well as some spectacular views of the coastline and the Puig Mayor dominating the landscape at 1445m/4740ft.

Begin the walk at K2.2 on the road to La Calobra (there is plenty of room to leave a car). There's a large stone platform here, which was to be the base of a furnicular down to the cove of La Calobra — a plan which was abandoned.

From the stone wall, facing the Puig Mayor, bear up slightly to the right, where you will find a wide track. Cross this, and continue straight up ahead, where, a minute later, the narrow rocky path begins by the side of a young wild olive tree, and a rock splashed with red paint. Start climbing up the slope, heading for the electricity pylons,

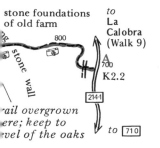

and later following alongside an old water channel. By about **15min** you'll have passed an old sheep hold and found a gap in the stone wall. Walk through, and you're on the northern slopes of the Puig Mayor, where the way levels out. From here there are excellent views of the coast near La Calobra over on

the right. You can see the old *atalaya* on the hilltop across the valley, and the road ribboning down to the cove far below.

Pass a small spring at **25min** (dry in summer) and in **30min** go through a gate in a stone wall. Down right are the stone foundations of an old farm. From here an old stone trail leads towards Bini valley. A few minutes along from the gate, you can see the steep slopes of the mighty Puig Mayor towering majestically above you to the left. There are not many trees in this area, which is characterised by bare and jagged rocks alternating with wind-blown long golden grass, forming a series of lonely hills and valleys that reach down to the coastline. However, you will pass by a small group of oaks standing bravely on the bare slope at about **35min**.

This is a good spot to end the short walk with a picnic, or perhaps you'll decide to go on for another few minutes, as far as the Font de Sa Baume. Here you can stop for a refreshing drink (except in July and August, when the spring *may* be dry).

Continuing along, the way is now an old moss-covered trail, lined with bracken. Meet more gates at **50min**: just past here is the wide earth track between the C710 and the Bini farms. (For the Alternative walk, follow the track up left; it will take you through lovely oak woods on the Coll d'es Carscolers ridge, to the C710 (900m below the tunnel). Be sure to have transport waiting! — see **STOP PRESS**, p168.)

Our continuing (right-hand) track leads down into the valley of Bini. Walking along here, some five minutes later, you will be able to look down into this beautiful valley, unbelievably green in winter and early spring, contrasting with the bareness of the surrounding mountains. The houses of Bini Petit and Bini Grand lie sheltered and protected from the raw sea winds of winter, whilst their sheep graze undisturbed on the rich green pastures of this fertile area.

We can walk as far as the farmhouses, going through the gate (**1h** into the walk), and turning left through the second gate just before the buildings, continuing on to the stream. A quaint little bridge crosses the stream here, and then the way continues up the rocky slope to where the house of Bini Grand hides in the trees. There used to be a continuing trail from Bini Grand, over the thickly wooded mountain, through the Coll de Bini, as far as Montcaire. However, it's been completely lost through disuse — partly because the owners of Montcaire will not permit anyone to walk over their land (see also Walk 8). So we'll return by the same route, or perhaps make for the Coll de Carscolers and the C710 — collecting fossils as we go!

11 CANALETAS OLD AND NEW: CUBER · GORG BLAU · ES PRAT · LA CANALETA DE MASSANELLA · TOSSALS · CUBER

Distance: 11km/6¾mi; 4½h

Grade: fairly easy: level walking along new aqueduct path, followed by gentle ups and downs (on generally rocky paths)

Equipment: stout walking shoes or boots, sunhat, picnic, plastic bottle with water purifying tablets, anorak in winter

How to get there: hired car to the Cuber reservoir (or taxi from Soller or Inca); but see also **STOP PRESS**, page 168
To return: See 'Language hints', page 157, if you wish to ask a taxi driver to wait for you at the Cuber reservoir, or to return for you

Short walk: Cuber reservoir to Canaleta de Massanella and return (A→B→A: 7.5km/4½mi; 2¾h); grade and equipment as above

The faint tinkling of sheep bells in the distance, the wind whispering its secrets in the valley, and the restful flow of moving waters are the only sounds that penetrate the impressive silence of the mountains in this beautiful part of the *sierra*. And even these sounds disappear once you've reached the mountainside of Tossals Verts, where the silence is almost as wonderful as the majesty of the peaks.

Start the walk at the Cuber reservoir on the C710. Walk east on the main road for a few minutes, to find the crossing of the modern aqueduct. Some 30m (yds) further along, a track leads up right to a path beside this *canaleta* (you can join *at* the aqueduct crossing, but there's a marshy spot here which the track avoids). At first you'll meet a couple of wet patches on the path; but there are detours round them, or else you can cross on large stones.

Following along, hopefully beside rushing waters, you'll find that this level, easy path quickly rises well above the C710 and in **10min** you'll have a superb overview of the Gorg Blau reservoir. Several good promontories overlook it, but the best one for picnicking is reached in half an hour, on a rocky outcropping shaded by evergreen oaks.

This modern *canaleta* takes water piped up from the Gorg Blau (you can see the pipe at the western end of that reservoir) and carries it to the Cuber, from where it is piped to Palma.

Having passed a couple of small 'flyovers' on the channel, in **45min** walking you'll come to a proper bridge over the aqueduct. Cross it, and start up a wide and rocky path. Soon meet a stone wall, where you can pass through a gap (but if it has been repaired, there's a hand-made ladder to help you over). Just beyond the wall, to the left, is a geographical stone.

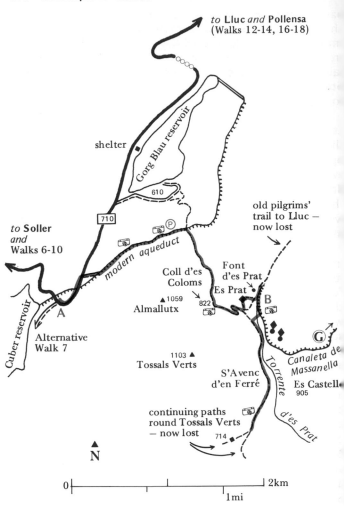

to **Lluc** and **Pollensa**
(Walks 12-14, 16-18)

shelter

Gorg Blau reservoir

610

710

old pilgrims'
trail to Lluc —
now lost

to **Soller**
and
Walks 6-10

modern aqueduct

Coll d'es
Coloms

Font
d'es Prat

Es Prat

B

P

Cuber reservoir

A

Alternative
Walk 7

▲1059
Almallutx

822

Canaleta de
Massanella

G

1103 ▲
Tossals Verts

S'Avenc
d'en Ferré

Torrente

Es Castell
905

continuing paths
round Tossals Verts
— now lost

d'es Prat

714

▲
N

0   2km

1mi

Landscapes of Mallorca © 1984

We soon approach a pass, the Coll d'es Coloms, at 822m, the highest point of the walk. From here the Puig de Massanella rises in the east some 500m/1650ft above us.

Then, at **1h** into the walk, another geographical stone on the right bears the numbers 802, 092. This may refer to the height above sea level, since it's placed about 20 metres below the pass.

At **1h10min** the old farmhouse of Es Prat comes into view, half hidden amongst the trees. Climb the gate and pass by the abandoned corral. The main path continues ahead, but be sure to fork up left by the first *sitja* on a smaller path. This leads to the front of the Es Prat house, from where you have a splendid view of the distant mountain of Randa on the far horizon, across the plain between other mountains — an original and picturesque backcloth for a photograph.

Continuing on past the house, rejoin the main path and at **1h20min** you will find the Font d'es Prat de Massanella, the spring which feeds the Canaleta de Massanella. A large, open clearing, with plenty of shade from the ubiquitous evergreen oaks, invites us to lay down our rucksacks and drink plentifully from the crystal-clear, sparkling waters that flow from this ancient well. Right down inside the well, the date 1748 is engraved in the stonework, the year in which the construction of this old *canaleta* was begun.

The Canaleta de Massanella underwent 'modernisation' in 1983: now, like most other watercourses on Mallorca, its singing waters are piped in aluminium tubing. Whether for reasons of sanitation, or to prevent evaporation, it's all the same to both walkers and lovers of the countryside: we have lost one of the island's most enchanting beauty spots. There was a great outcry in the local papers from conservationists, but on Mallorca, as everywhere else, it is almost impossible to halt the wheels of 'progress'.

The history of the *canaleta* is interesting. The work is attributed to a Montserrat Fontanet, a Mallorcan pig farmer employed on the Massanella farmholding during the 18th century. The owner of this large property had expressly brought engineers from France, England, Italy and the Spanish mainland, to plan and execute the channelling of water from the Prat spring. All these eminent engineers agreed that the feat was technically impossible, after which Señor Fontanet offered to do the job himself. His employer agreed to his suggestion, and the work was (reportedly) finished in two years' time — a record feat by any standards! History accounts that Señor Fontanet later wrote a book on agriculture; thus he was not altogether uncultured, as was reportedly said of him in earlier days. Whatever kind of man he may have been, this work of art is certainly a monument of which the Mallorcans are extremely proud.

Before you leave Es Prat, you may like to explore a bit on the old pilgrims' trail to Lluc: it passed the *font* and continued north of the Massanella peak. Unfortunately, the way is now completely lost north of Massanella (see also Walk 12).

Now double back on your tracks, to visit the *canaleta* itself. About 60m (yds) back from the spring, you'll see a three-pronged fork in the main route: at your left, a path crosses a stream; the main path goes straight ahead. We take the way that runs at a 45-degree angle between these two. The stream will be on our left as we follow this middle path. The old Canaleta de Massanella is hidden beneath our feet, but the stonework emerges to the surface some 300m (yds) further along — by some lovely pools. This is a superb place for picnicking, beside the running (overspill) waters, in the shade of oaks. The only disappointment is that the water in the *canaleta* is no longer free-flowing, and only earth, covering the tubing, is to be seen between the stone edges of the channel.

It used to be a wonderful adventure to follow the *canaleta* from here: one climbed the high stone wall of Es Molinot (the old mill, the remains of which may still be seen down in the valley) and had to proceed very carefully along a very narrow stretch for about five minutes, as the channel rounded the side of the mountain. If you're not subject to vertigo, and you're sure-footed, about five minutes along from the Es Molinot wall, you will be able to see the arched aqueduct that carries the *canaleta* across a ravine — still a beautiful sight. The channel continues from there, through waterfalls and tunnels, into the village of Mancor del Valle, about six kilometres southeast.

Now let's make for the old farm at Tossals Verts, where we can picnic on a grassy slope, surrounded by high mountains on all sides. If you've ventured along the water channel, turn back, climb over the wall, and make a descent into the valley of S'Avenc d'en Ferré, following alongside the old stone wall, crossing the Es Prat stream, and making your way up the opposite mountainside, where you'll find the path that rounds Tossals Verts.

Head south, and a large boulder appears below in the valley, called Es Castellot. Beyond it, and to the right, one can explore the caves in the hillside. But beware: the descent is difficult, and there is no path. The views from this mountainside path are very good: the village of Selva lies peacefully across the Massanella valley, and the Puig de Inca and the mountains of Artá far to the east can be seen. Soon (2h30min) see the old stone wall of the *finca* of Tossals Verts, a long-abandoned farm. Passing through a gap in the wall, you will soon find a wide grassy area on the open mountainside, by an old well — the Font de Sa Basola — another ideal spot for lunch.

Distance: 12km/7¼mi; 5h
Grade: **G**; strenuous. Scrambling over rocks, **danger of vertigo**, and possibility of sudden thick mists; path also difficult to find at times
Equipment: walking boots, long trousers, cardigans, sunhat, anorak, whistle, torch, picnic, plastic bottle with water purifying tablets
How to get there: 🚌 to Inca
Depart Palma 09.00; arriva Inca 09.35, to connect with 🚐 to Lluc, which waits outside station and departs 09.45; arrives Lluc 10.20
NB: for *this* walk, do not go into Lluc, but ask to be put off at the petrol station before Lluc ('estación de servicio de Lluc, por favor')
To return: 🚐 from Lluc (or petrol station) to Inca: departs Lluc 18.00; arrives Inca 18.30. 🚌 departs Inca 19.00; arrives Palma 19.35
NB: See **STOP PRESS**, p168, if you're staying in Soller or Pollensa
Short walk: as far as you like along the path of the main walk, perhaps as far as the first indication stones (A→B→A: 5km/3mi; 1¾h *return*); equipment as above (except torch); no guide necessary

The Puig de Massanella is that double-peaked, high rock mountain, in the northern stretch of the *sierra*, visible from many parts of the island. The second highest peak on Mallorca, it reaches up 1352m (4435ft). And about 150m below the summit, the freshwater spring of the Font de S'Avenc, hidden deep in the mountainside, bubbles fresh, cool, filtered water almost all the year round.

The walk begins at the petrol station south of Lluc. About 150m (yds) below the station, find green gates on your right; a block of stone to the left is engraved 'Puig de Massanella'. Go through the gates and take the first turning right (a short cut). Right again, 20m or so up, by a rock with a red paint daub. You will soon rejoin the main route, where you'll see a large, red paint-marked rock. From here, take the narrow path up to the right (a continuation of the short cut), again rejoining the main track. Now along the main route, you will meet a gate at **15min**. Climb over a stile at the right. Soon you'll see the farm buildings of Comafreda on your right, in open fields across the stream.

At **25min**, on approaching the old gate in the stone wall, turn up to the left just before the gate, following the marks on the wall itself. The way to the right leads to the farmhouse, and the trail straight ahead through the gates is the old pilgrims' route between Lluc and Soller (see Walks 7 and 11), unfortunately now impassable around Massanella.

Our rocky path up left heads through oaks, marked with red paint. At **30min**, go over the remains of an old stone wall, almost in ruins, and a minute later, continue straight on (another short cut). Climb up ancient stony steps, turning left where the paint splashes indicate. Rejoin the main way in five minutes, and turn up left, following red arrows.

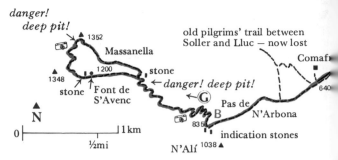

At **40min** turn right, still following the main route, and
on arriving at a small clearing (just by an old stone *refugio*)
turn up the rocky slope towards the left, where you will see
a large red arrow on the rock, pointing upwards. Red paint
marks now guide us up through the Pas de N'Arbona.

Ten minutes later, you will come to another clearing. On
the left, there is the Puig de N'Alí (1038m), before we come
to the two large indication stones. 'Puig de Massanella'
clearly engraved on one of them, indicates a sharp turn to
the right from here, following the red arrows up through
the trees, and bearing right. Now the path begins to wind
up rather more steeply. From here onwards, keep a sharp
lookout for the red paint marks, as the path can be difficult
to distinguish from time to time, until we reach the summit
in about another 90 minutes.

At **1h**, you'll see a large red II painted on the rock, on a
bend in the path. Further on up, the view begins to attract
our attention, and it is advisable to stop for a breather from
time to time, to admire the splendid scenery. The plain
stretches out below, down to the southern coastline and the
city of Palma, where the wide bay shimmers in the sun and
a misty haze hides the horizon.

Passing between large boulders, trees and long grasses,
our path has become very rocky indeed. Always keep a keen
lookout for the red paint marks! At **1h25min** at the Avenc
del Camí, a mountain 'crossroads', there is a small hole down
to a cave on the right of the path. Careful, it's very deep!
Now find the indication stone, which directs two ways: to
the Font de S'Avenc straight on, and to the summit, up the
rocky slope. It you wish to go straight to the peak, the path
is quite easily seen from here; but coming down to the
fountain, it is difficult to see the red marks on the steep
descent. So let's make the tour in a clockwise direction,
first visiting the fountain and taking a breather. When we
reach the summit, our return path will be easy to find.

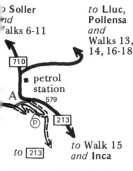

to Soller
nd
alks 6-11

710

petrol
station
579
A

P 213

to 213

to Lluc,
Pollensa
and
Walks 13,
14, 16-18

to Walk 15
and Inca

Landscapes of Mallorca © 1984

Our path to the fountain climbs two stony slopes, the way indicated by red paint and small piles of rocks, generally bearing left. At **1h35min**, come to a wide open rock slope and head up right towards the large and solitary oak. Past here, a long, high and wide stretch of treeless jagged rocks and boulders is seen ahead, before the red paint marks take us to the Font de S'Avenc (**1h45min**). This is a marvellous place. Stone steps lead deep down into the mountain, like the entrance to an Aladdin's Cave. We wind down into the cool, dark interior, where the spring bubbles out of the rocks into a stone well. You'll need a torch — it's pitch black. Take on water, before assaulting the summit.

An indication stone at the fountain shows the way up, and there's a good deal of clambering over high rocks. One feels infinitely minute, nothing but a speck of humanity, slowly crawling up this massive rocky mountain, like a tiny ant labouring over a boulder. It is also rather discouraging to discover that, once over the brow ahead, the peaks still remain quite a way ahead!

Still, the way is easily followed — even if tiring — the red-painted rocks being easily seen from this direction. A host of wild chamomile plants ekes out an arid existence here amongst the rocks, and very occasionally you'll see a wild peony, the only splash of gaiety amongst the monotonous grey rocks and dusty scrubs.

In **2h30min** you will reach the top! And the panorama is of course worth every minute of the effort. The whole of the island lies below you, a magical landscape of mountains, hills and valleys, surrounded by the blue Mediterranean. You're on the highest accessible peak on Mallorca, now that the Puig Mayor is closed because of the radar station.

In your wonder and admiration, don't forget to be careful — just below the peak is one of the deepest snow pits on the island — it must go down almost 20m (50ft)!

Looking down towards the left, facing the plain, you will be able to see a tiny path way below on a sort of flat tableland area at the foot of the rocky slope. We'll make for this route, as we begin the descent. It's really fairly easy, jumping from rock to boulder, boulder to rock, and takes about twenty minutes to reach the path. And from here back, the way is very easy to follow, right to the Lluc road.

13 AROUND THE PUIG ROIG: LLUC · MOSSA COLL D'ELS ASES · COSCONAS · LLUC

Distance: 19km/11½mi; 7h

Grade: moderate, over well-defined, but sometimes very stony paths; some **danger of vertigo** by Coll d'els Ases and beyond

Equipment: stout shoes or boots, anorak, sunhat, picnic, plastic bottle with water purifying tablets, cardigan

How to get there: see Walk 12 (for Lluc); see also **STOP PRESS**, p16

Short walk: Lluc to Ca'n Pontico and return (A→B→A: 8km/5mi; 2¾h); easy; take stout shoes, picnic, water, sunhat. Follow the lane to the left of the monastery (between the monastery and the bar-café); picnic near the roadside — not on cultivation

Alternative walk: Lluc to Cosconás and return (A→C→A: 13km/7¾mi; 5h); equipment as above; start out as in Short walk; easy

The long and winding path that rounds the Puig Roig (the Red Mountain) offers some magnificent panorama along the wild and rugged coastline near La Calobra, and by far the island's best views of the Puig Mayor. Although this is a very long walk, it is certainly not difficult, and anyone stoutly shod with plenty of stamina can do it.

Start out from Lluc as in Walk 14 (see page 114), to join the C710 in **25min**. Follow the road to Mossa's gates (**1h**) (See also **STOP PRESS**, page 168: you may be able to get bus from Lluc to Mossa, saving one hour.) Go in the Mossa gates, and follow the earth track (ignoring a path to the left) Continuing on towards the right, some 50m (yds) further along, you will pass through another gate. Looking to the left, the red cliffsides of the long and high Puig Roig now dominate the landscape. Passing through another gate in ten minutes, the still air is full of the delightful tinkling of countless sheepbells, as you approach Mossa's farm.

The track now leads slightly upwards, rounding the farm and passing another gateway. Walk quietly here, being as unprovocative as possible to the loudly-barking farm dogs Don't worry — they are all chained up, and they won't bother to keep up this cacaphony once you have gone through the gates to the left of the old house.

Now continue straight ahead, crossing a small patch of rocky terrain, where you will find the narrow, rocky path directly in front of you. Pass through the gap in an old stone wall and soon you will have some splendid views of the pretty little Mossa river valley gradually falling away below. As you come up to the pass, the Coll d'els Ases, the last lap rounds a steep cliffside — with some danger of vertigo. You'll reach the *coll* at **1h50min**, and soon catch your first glimpse of the sea. The panorama from this saddle at 627m/2055ft is wonderful. Behind, to the south

ast, the Puig Tomir (Walk 14) thrusts its wide, triangular-
haped peak into the sky. On your left, the Sierra de la
Mola del Teix — at its most beautiful when covered with
now — edges the landscape with majesty.

On the right, almost treeless mountains undulate down
o an indigo sea. Just behind these mountains is the *come-
ero, the vultures' feeding ground. Because of the lack of
uitable food for this endangered species, ICONA takes a
veekly supply of carrion, thus ensuring the survival of these
eautiful birds. There are few left, but this is one of the
reas where you are most likely to spot their enormous,
lark silhouettes, with the characteristic pointed tails.

The rocky and exciting path continues now for over two
ours more, rounding the whole of the north side of the
'uig Roig, with magnificent views over the famous abutment,
he Morro de Sa Vaca, jutting out just before the bay of
.a Calobra, and the Morro d'els Bordils, where the ancient
vatchtower of Lluc has looked out over the sea for cen-
uries. (There used to be a path to this *atalaya*, but the way
s no longer safe.) Further along, we have the island's most
lramatic view of its highest peak, the mighty Puig Mayor.

Pass between some huge solitary pines growing on the
are mountainside, and in five minutes you will arrive at a
ong, low stone wall which runs down the hillside as far
is the old house of the *carabineros*. To reach this old civil
;uards' house, you'll have to clamber down the hillside
eside the wall — it takes about fifteen minutes. The civil
;uard, although supposedly here to guard the coast, spent
nost of their time trading illegally with smugglers. By night
ocal workers carried great sacks of tobacco, coffee and
ugar smuggled ashore from Africa, along this very same
ath to the north of the Red Mountain — it's the old
mugglers' route that we've been following from Mossa.

Having explored for a while, take the path that leads
way through the gate just down in front of the house.
Continue along here for about five minutes, and you will
come to an enclosure, as the path makes a U-turn. Climb
ip a few metres on the farther side and just behind a
corrugated roof covering a water tank you'll find a spring
(best to use water purifying tablets here) coming out of a
mall tunnel in the hillside. Slightly up to the right of this
ou will find a flat grassy patch shaded by a group of pines,
he perfect spot for a picnic and a rest, enjoying the magnificent views of Puig Mayor and the high *sierra*.

The return journey begins on the same route, at the
oot of the spring, turning left after descending from the

picnic area, and following along a wide but rocky path.
Take no notice of the red arrow on a rock pointing uphill
ten minutes further along (unless you are making the alternative walk and wish to visit the civil guards' house — this is
only a shortcut to it). Pass through two sets of gates to see
the pretty olive-covered slopes going down into the Lluc
stream valley. Further down, you'll see the *entreforc*, where
the waters from the Torrente de Lluc and Sa Fosca unite to
form the Torrente de Pareis (our Walk 9).

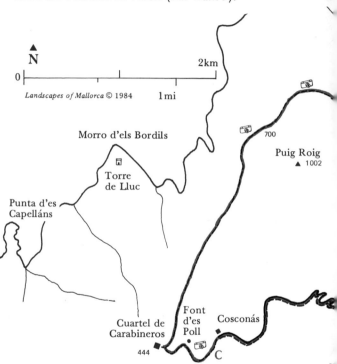

At about **4h45min**, passing through more gates, you will
see the amazing old houses of Cosconás, built into the
natural caves in the mountainside. From Cosconás back to
Lluc the track is flat and wide — very comfortable for
walking. It winds on down the south side of the Puig Roig,
through farmlands, apple orchards, almond trees and some
terraces populated by thousand-year-old olive trees, twisted
by age into highly imaginative forms.
    Keep always to the main track, passing by the gates of
the *finca* of Sa Plana on the left, and soon after, an old
abandoned house with a sun dial on its walls. Neat stone

walls and wrought iron gates, through which many well-kept gardens may be glimpsed, mark your approach to Ca'n Pontico. Cross a small bridge over the (generally dry) Mossa stream and then stride out through flat open fields before you start to wind your way up to Lluc, where a large cross is visible at the top of the hill. Making a final effort on these last tiring uphill bends, you soon reach a tarmac road — a continuation of the track. It leads right into the monastery forecourt and the oasis of a bar-café (7h).

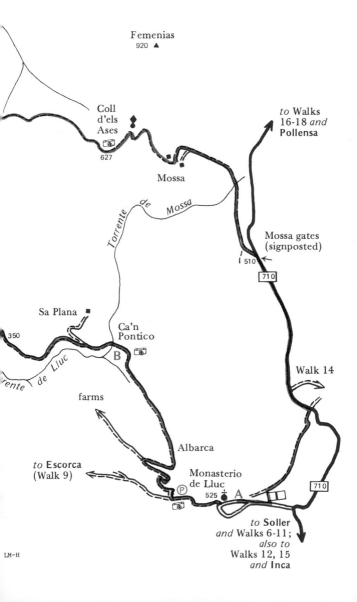

14 A SCRAMBLE UP THE PUIG TOMIR

Distance: 12km/7¼mi; 5h

Grade: Ⓖ; **only for experts.** Two potentially dangerous scree-covered areas must be crossed, much clambering over rocks, **danger of vertigo**, possibility of sudden thick mists; do not attempt in winter

Equipment: walking boots, long trousers, sunhat, whistle, picnic, water, walking stick; cardigans, anorak and headgear in cool weather

How to get there: see Walk 12 (for Lluc); see also **STOP PRESS**, p168

Short walk: Lluc to Finca Binifaldó and return (A→B→A: 5km/3mi; under 2h). Easy. Take sunhat, picnic, water and enjoy a woodland stroll; picnic spots abound, especially on the Binifaldó road

More a mountaineering adventure than a walk, this scramble is only for the sure-footed. But anyone can enjoy the pleasant woodland stroll during the first hour, by following the tarmac lane to the foot of Tomir.

If the weather is dry, but not too hot, and you're really fit, off we go. The fantastic views from Tomir's peak (1107m/3630ft) — the third highest on the island — make the effort well worth while. A magnificent panorama of hills, mountains, plains, wide bays and coastline will unfold itself before your eyes — an eagle's eye view of Mallorca!

To start out, leave Lluc by the main gates. About 100m (yds) along the secondary road, find a wooden gate on the left. Turn in, and take the path to the right, through the football pitch and past the *fronton* courts. Now the way is a picturesque old track, winding gracefully through trees and rocks eroded into wonderfully whimsical shapes. We pass by a picnic and camping area, and at **25min** come out on the main C710. Turn left here, and walk for about 100m (yds) to the K17.4 stone. Here, on the right, are the gates to Binifaldó and a large wooden sign: 'Ministerio de Agricultura. Jefatura Principal de ICONA. Vivero Central de Manut'.

Turn into the lane (the old route to Pollensa) leading to ICONA's headquarters, and enjoy the gentle uphill stroll through well-kept woodlands and ever more wonderfully-formed rocks. In **35min** you'll meet two sets of green gates. Opt for the left-hand gate, and continue along the old Lluc—Pollensa road until a group of poplars announces your arrival at the *finca* of Binifaldó (**55min**). The old road continues on through the gates over left, just beyond the poplars.

Today's walk lies straight ahead, however: in **1h15min** you'll come to tall iron gates at the entrance to the water-bottling plant at Binifaldó fountain — watch out for heavily-laden lorries just as you pass through here.

Monasterio de Lluc

525

to **Soller**
and Walks 6-11;
also to
Walks 12, 15
and **Inca**

114

The path up Tomir mountain begins on the right, on the other side of the boundary fence, just by the gates. Follow up alongside the fence, and in about five minutes keep a very sharp eye out for the red arrow on the rock at ground level, pointing up to the right. It is easily missed, because the path alongside the fence continues ahead. We turn right, following a path winding up the mountainside. A minute later, another arrow points left, where the path bends sharply, and then turns up to the right again. Look out for the arrows which will guide you up through the trees, and later onto the rocky mountain.

Soon you'll come to the steep stony slope, the first scree area — said to be the remains of a glacier. **Extra care must be taken here, and do not attempt to cross the scree after a period of rain.** Only after you have safely crossed should you stop to admire the surrounding landscapes, the setting of so many other walks: the beautiful valley of Lluc, lying at the foot of the pine-covered mountains, the double peak of the Puig de Massanella, the enormous Puig Roig majestic on the cloud-studded horizon, and its close neighbour, the mighty Puig Mayor searing the heavens. It all leaves you quite breathless — apart from the climb!

Now we hike up the steep side of the cliff, up to a small pass. From here, Palma is visible on the south coast, and a

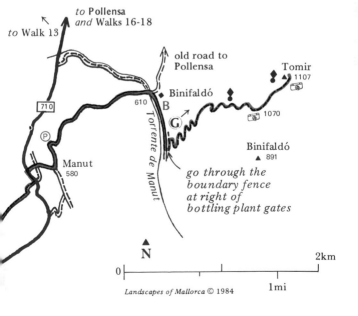

Landscapes of Mallorca © 1984

rest is advisable, not only to admire the views, but also to catch your breath before starting to climb the second scree area, where again **extra care is needed!**

The path follows up to the right, alongside the second scree area, where there are plenty of loose rocks. Then, at about **1h55min** into the walk, you will have to clamber over the rock face, after which the path is rather camouflaged as it crosses the rocky terrain. Head east, following the rocky way, and keeping the two peaks on your left — bearing right where, from time to time, you can see the red arrows on the rocks. At about **2h5min** go left by a pile of rocks, and continue on upwards, keeping left, following the arrows up to the second, higher peak. You should arrive here at about **2h15min** into the walk.

The view is really fantastic, but there is more to come! Keep on, bearing left, for what seems an endless clamber over rocks and low rosemary-scented scrub, towards the highest part of the *puig*, where Scouts have placed an iron cross. There are arrows and piles of rocks to guide you, but it is easy enough if you just head left over the various peaks (being careful of the steep drops to the left) until you eventually reach the true, 1107m-high summit, at **2h45min**.

Here breath-taking views of the island's landscapes will hold you enthralled, as you contemplate the 'world' beneath your feet. Perhaps this is the best vantage point on the island to appreciate the beauty of the bays and headlands in the northeast, the landscapes of Walks 18—25.

Enjoy your picnic lunch before you make a final tour of exploration up here. There's an old snow-pit down below the cross — be careful; it's quite deep. From here, allow about an hour to return to the gates at Binifaldó, and an another hour and a quarter back to Lluc.

23
24

25
26
27

28

29

30

5 CAMPANET · BINIATRO · SES FONS · AUCANELLA · BINIBONA · CAIMARI

Distance: 16km/9¾mi; under 6h

Grade: moderate, with a gentle, steady uphill climb

Equipment: stout shoes (boots in winter), whistle, insect repellant, long-sleeved shirt and long trousers (see notes in text), cardigan and anorak, as well as waterproof trousers in winter, picnic, water

How to get there: 🚌 to Inca
Departs Palma 09.00; arrives Inca 09.35
Taxi from Inca station: ask for 'Cuevas de Campanet'
NB: on Sundays *only*, there is a bus direct to Campanet at 09.00, but the walk from Campanet to the Oratorio will take about 1 hour
To return: 🚌 from Caimari to Inca. This is the Lluc bus; last departure from Lluc 18.00; passes Caimari 18.15; arrives Inca 18.30
🚌 from Inca to Palma: departs 19.00; arrives 19.35

Short/Alternative walks: use the map to explore as you like from either Campanet or Caimari, making easy walks (stout shoes, sunhat, picnic, water). There's a bus to Campanet at 12.45, and at 09.00 *Sundays only*, with convenient return times (see Timetable p159). The Lluc bus passes Caimari, and the convenient Selva buses bring you to the PM213 just 2km below Caimari. See Timetables p159-61. From Campanet (**A**), visit the Oratorio (**B**) and the caves or the Font d'els Cipresos (**C**); from Caimari (**D**) visit Binibona (**E**)

A beautiful walk, the Campanet—Caimari route begins in the attractive woodland area of the foothills just below the Puig Tomir (Walk 14). Tall and dominant evergreen oaks, the occasional eucalyptus, and delicately-perfumed *Erica multiflora* grow in quiescent harmony on the sloping hillsides, serenaded by the song of the nightingale in spring, and dappled by shafts of golden sunlight. Pine forests further up suddenly open out onto a wide *pla*, or tableland, surrounded on all sides by the mountains, and the route descends later through dense undergrowth and thick forest to the pretty smallholding of Binibona, from where a narrow country lane ribbons its way over low hills to the mountain village of Caimari. Although the walk is fairly long, it's not too taxing — especially on a coolish day — and the beauty and stillness of these woodlands and artistically-landscaped hillsides, colourful portraits of Mallorca's flora and fauna, are ample compensation.

Start the walk on the old Campanet—Pollensa road, in front of the Oratorio San Miguel, a pretty thirteenth century church just to the south of the entrance to the famous Cuevas de Campanet. Continue straight ahead on this road, keeping left at a fork. Soon you'll see the large old house of Biniatró up ahead on the hillside. You'll pass two old cypress trees and a small ruin on your right, before you spot the track up to Biniatró (**30min**), which begins almost opposite the ruins of an old *casita*.

This old track leads up between two low stone walls. It crosses the *torrente* and then goes over open fields, climbing gradually up into the foothills. Soon you will arrive at the enormous old farmstead of Biniatró (**45min**), once the home of the several families needed to tend the lands and harvest the crops of this extensive *finca*. If you are lucky enough to find the shutters open on the third window along from the door, you will be able to see the enormous wooden screws on the ancient olive-press that produced oil in this once-thriving community.

The way continues through the beautiful farmlands, past the gardens on the right (now sadly abandoned) and a multitude of olive trees up on the rocky slopes. Then you'll pass through the iron gate to the Ses Fons holding (ignore the 'Prohibido el paso' sign; you have right of way (to the Font d'els Cipresos).

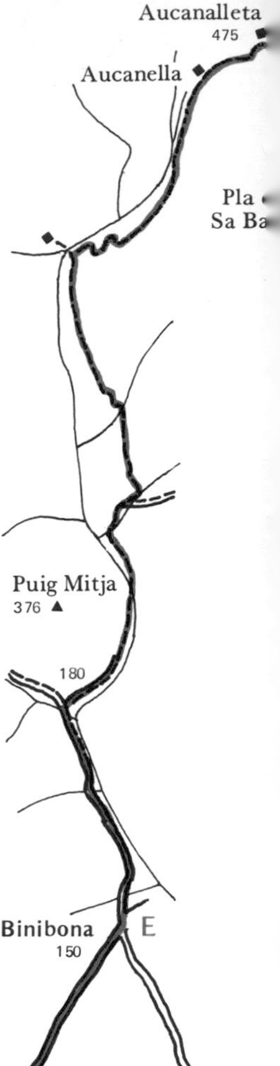

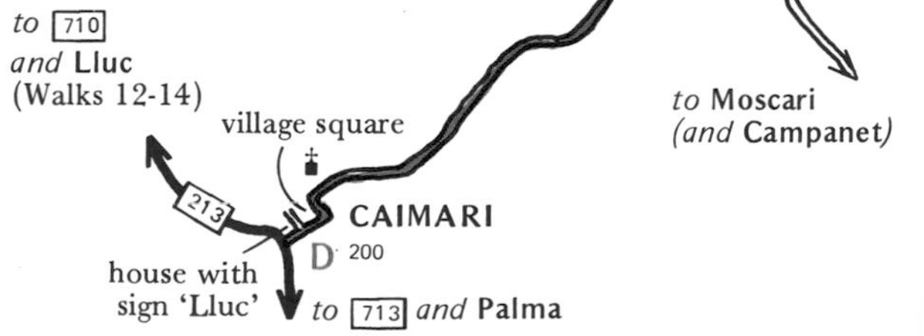

Aucanalleta
475

Aucanella

Pla
Sa Ba

Puig Mitja
376 ▲

180

Binibona   E
150

to 710
and Lluc
(Walks 12-14)

to Moscari
(and Campanet*)*

village square

CAIMARI

273   D   200

house with
sign 'Lluc'   *to* 713 *and* Palma

Cypress trees grow alongside the stream in the valley on the left, and the surrounding fields, as green as emeralds in winter, provide pasture for grazing sheep. Ignore a small path bending down to the left just by an iron gate. Five minutes later, go through the gates ahead of you, and take the track immediately to the left (through another gate),

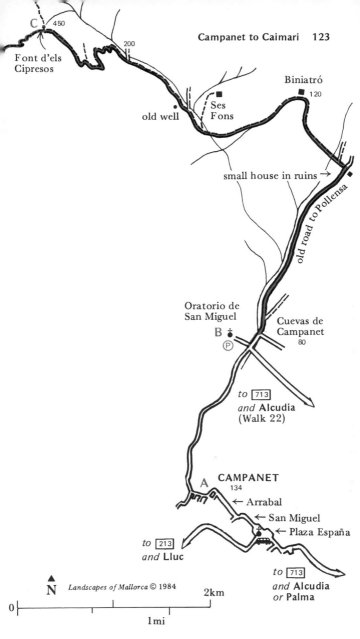

crossing the stream bed. Then bear right past an old oak, towards a *sitja*. The track is easily visible from here: it leads into the woods. Through the trees, you will soon be able to see the big house of Ses Fons on the hillside over right. Keeping to the main route, and ignoring various *caminos forrestales* branching off, you'll pass by an old well at the side of a long-disused *sitja*. Here, the delicate perfume of the *Erica multiflora* wafts on the breeze, and you'll recognise the odd strawberry tree and mastic bushes. The bell-like song of the nightingale echoes clearly through the tall oaks, and the mating call of the Hoopoe rings out incessantly — all tell-tale signs of Nature's most magnificent adventure, spring — if you make the walk at the right time of the year.

As we continue uphill, high rocky mountains soon appear on our right. Ignoring all offshoots of our moss-edged trail, we pass through a gate, with the stream still on our right. Then we leave the stream to climb the wooded slopes in a series of bends, until we reach a small clearing on the left, dominated by an enormous oak, hundreds of years old. Its branches — thicker than most tree trunks — spread out wide and fork upwards in a multitude of smaller *ramas*, reaching many feet up towards the sunlight.

Soon the oaks give way to pines and thicker undergrowth, and then we can see the distant bay of Alcudia and the marshlands of the Albufera lying on the horizon behind us to the right. Up ahead, the high and bare rocks of the Puig Tomir seem very close. A few minutes later (**2h**) we come to the Font d'els Cipresos, named for the abundant cypresses growing round this well. At the spring, the continuing right-hand path only leads up to the olive slopes; we take the path up left, which winds through pines and ferns towards the *pla*. (Be careful not to take the small path leading off right a bit further up; it only returns to the well.) Go through an old wooden gate, and continue straight ahead, across the open fields of the *planicie*. This wide, high, open space is wonderful after the long climb through the woods; breathe in the clear, cool mountain air and admire your breath-takingly beautiful surroundings.

The old abandoned house of Aucanalleta lies ahead. Cross the broken stone wall and head towards the house (there's no track here). You may like to picnic at the house (**2h30min**), overlooking the pretty valley. From here there's no easily-discerned path for the next stretch of the walk, so follow the notes carefully! The second house of Aucanella is our next landmark. From the front of the house at Aucanalleta, take the *right-hand* opening in the stone wall of the patio, and follow down left, going down a rough path. Go through a small gate at the bottom (ignoring the 'Coto privado de caza' sign — this only means 'private hunting ground'). Continue over the rocks, straight ahead downhill, following the narrow path down to the open fields just below the house of Aucanella.

Our route does not visit the Aucanella house, but stays in the open fields well below it, bearing slightly left and making for a gap in the stone wall seen up ahead. Pass through the opening in the stone wall, and bear left across the wide open field, with the low stone wall running alongside on the left. Keep the pine-clad slope on your left, and the valley to the right. Head for the lowest part of the horizon, where you will come to a wire fence. There is a good picnic spot here, just to the left, where trees provide shade and the wall a back-rest.

Now begin the descent into the valley, by going through the large hole in the wire fence (4m to the left of the tree), and turning left along the rocky path. Careful not to miss it! It's fairly camouflaged amongst the rocks. This narrow path leads you on down, through the thick undergrowth, between large rocks and boulders — the valley is still on your right. (This might be a good time to put on the long-leeved shirt and long trousers you brought.)

On arriving at some large oak trees, the way continues ahead on a narrow path. A wire fence is close by at the right, and you can spot a house down right, across the stream bed. At a second group of oaks, the path heads down and slightly right amongst the rocks. Continuing on ahead and slightly downwards, you should be able to follow this overgrown path, quite narrow, but later widening out, through the trees.

Keeping to the ever-descending path, in a few minutes you'll pass the way across the stream to the house you glimpsed earlier on (3h40min). Keep on ahead, to go through the dilapidated old gate of the abandoned farm. From here, the path leads on through dense undergrowth, and if you have not yet put on long trousers and a long-leeved shirt, this is the time to do so — especially in late spring or warmer weather. Watch out for horrible little *arrapatas* — ticks — which would love to get a chance to attach themselves to you. They can only be got rid of by burning them out with a cigarette end, or a visit to the doctor. They have a special predilection for the scalp.

But soon this stretch is behind us, and a beautiful, deep and rugged valley opens up on our right, as the stony path starts to climb upwards. We go through another gate, and the way flattens out and leads through a small pass. Beyond here, there's a magnificent view of the plain. An enormous boulder planted in the foreground makes this a good place for a bit of photography. Standing beside this huge rock, you can see the deep valley, thick with pines, below.

Continuing the descent, we arrive at a large open clearing and take the path to the right through the woods. Ten minutes later, the path runs right into a *torrente*, but turn down along the stream bed, towards the left (plenty of stepping stones if there is water), for about 100m (yds) where the path re-emerges on the right. The way is now much better walking, by the high, pine-wooded cliff and the stream on the left. Ignore the small *camino forresta* across the stream on your left; a couple of minutes later, we come to a large green gate: go through, but if you find it locked, you will have to climb the low stone wall and fence to the left. The way now crosses an open area, with the woods receding away to the right.

Follow the well-worn, red earth track until you come to a second green gate. Past here, turn left down a lane — which is soon tarmac-surfaced — and you'll soon come to Binibona (**5h20min**), where old farm buildings and elegant modern houses mingle together, oblivious of class distinctions. The lane then takes a turn to the right and becomes a tarmac country road. Continue straight ahead here (the small country lane leading down to the left goes to the village of Moscari).

This narrow road, bordered by wild asparagus bushes and surrounded by rolling countryside, winds its way lazily over hills for another twenty-five minutes. You'll arrive at Caimari in about **6h** walking at most. Once into the village, make your way down the narrow streets, past the village square, towards the main road. Here you can stop the Lluc—Inca bus anywhere, as it passes through the village.

Distance: from Mortitx to Sa Cova de Ses Bruixes and return: 8km/ ¾mi; 4h; to return via El Torrente de Mortitx add 1½km (1h)

Grade: very rocky, wild terrain makes the going a bit tricky, and the path is often difficult to distinguish. Only experts, with a guide, should attempt to return via the *torrente* and only in very dry conditions: some strenuous clambering over slippery rocks is involved

Equipment: walking boots, whistle, long trousers, water, picnic, cardigans and arorak with hood in winter; sunhat in hot weather

How to get there: 🚌 to Pollensa and return (all details page 130) *Taxi from Pollensa to Mortitx and return* (taxi rank is by bus stop); ask the driver to return for you — see 'Language hints', page 157, no later than 30 minutes before the return bus
NB: see also **STOP PRESS**, page 168

Short walk: as far as you like along the course of the main walk; the 'wild west' setting of fantastic rock formations surrounds you almost from the start; stout shoes will suffice for a short walk

The Rafal de Ariant Trail is an ancient, narrow, rocky path over some of the most wild and fantastic, rugged mountain terrain on Mallorca. The scenery along here is almost phantasmagoric — the shapes and strange formations of huge boulders and wind-sculptured rocks, strewn over the uneven surface of the mountains creating a wild and savage panorama. And an eerie silence, broken only by the wind and the occasional cry of some wild bird, lends an aura of mysticism to this unspoilt and uncivilised part of the *sierra*. Finally, the sheer coastal cliffs are reached, with drops of 200m/650ft straight down into the sea. Here the steep escarpment is riddled with fantastic huge caves carved out of the rock faces by the elements, and the sea foams white and savage on the rocks below.

It's a walk with a difference! And all the more exciting on a windy, winter's day, when the clouds cast their moving shadows over the mountains, so accentuating the shapes and shadows of the rocks. If you go in warm weather, a sunhat is a must — there is very little shade, except at the old abandoned houses of Rafal de Ariant.

Leave the taxi at the Mortitx gates (if you come by car, these lie between the 10 and 11km markers on the C710; park well against the wall). **Start out** by passing two sets of gates and walking *past* the tennis court. Then go right through another gate at the left of a stone shed, and walk between two peach plantations up to another gate on the left (**10min**). Just beyond this gate is a small grassy area with a fig tree. Then the path leads slightly upwards, by large rocks and olive trees to another gate and a fork. At the left you will see a large marker stone, painted red, blue

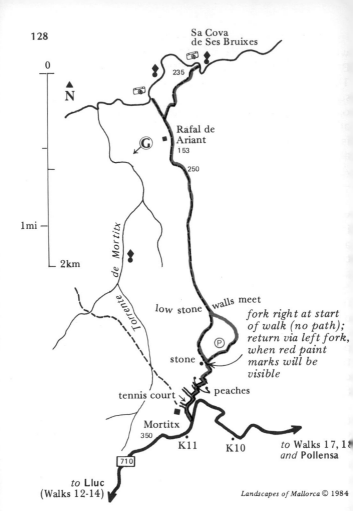

Sa Cova
de Ses Bruixes

235

Rafal de
Ariant
153

250

G

1mi

2km

Torrente de Mortitx

low stone walls *meet*

*fork right at start
of walk (no path);
return via left fork,
when red paint
marks will be
visible*

P

stone

tennis court

peaches

Mortitx
350

K11   K10   *to* Walks 17, 18
                   and Pollensa

710

to Lluc
(Walks 12-14)

Landscapes of Mallorca © 1984

and yellow. This marks our *return* path, but for the moment
we go straight on — only to find that our path disappears.
Head across open fields straight towards the coast — the
lowest point on the horizon. The terrain becomes more and
more rocky, till we come to a place where low stone walls
meet (**40min**). Go through the gate and continue along the
rocky path (sporadically marked with red paint). First it
climbs, and then starts downwards, where the going gets
more difficult when the path is not easily discernible.

At about **1h** turn up right 90°, by a rock with a hori-
zontal red bar, following small rock-pile markers. Then
at **1h10min** bear right 90° again, by a red-painted rock.
As you climb the rocky slope, you might like to turn
round for a view of the impressive landscapes behind you

with the Puig Tomir (Walk 14) high on the western horizon. Black vultures are often seen circling in this area. By about 1h20min, you'll be able to glimpse the sea; then this old *senda* dips down and crosses a flattish area. Go through an opening in an old stone wall and, a little later, continue along the path that bends to the left. (The way to the right is blocked by a pile of rocks.) The route now winds down an impressive cliffside to the abandoned houses of Rafal de Ariant (under 2h), where you may find some useful items — salt, matches, etc — left behind by other hikers.

From here it's only a short walk to the cliffs, perhaps with a goshawk or two circling overhead for company. There is some danger of vertigo near the edge; the drops to the sea are very sheer. Here the scenery is one of natural beauty: the cliffsides are full of caves of varying shapes and sizes, and the sea beats furiously on the rocks on a windy day.

To see the Cova de Ses Bruixes, follow over the plain from the house, bearing right, where a path of sorts leads down the coast towards a large boulder. From his huge rock follow on *very carefully* across the rocky slope to a stony platform, from where you will see the magnificent cave in the steep cliffside to the left. Its name means 'the witches' cave' in Mallorquin. This excursion takes about 20min from the house.

To return to Mortitx by the river bed — the *torrente* — take the path which runs down alongside the low stone wall, just near the house to the right, passing by some almond and fig trees, to where the stream bed lies between the huge rocks. You should only attempt this route back if the bed is dry, and it hasn't rained recently.

Follow the stream bed up through its rugged and beautiful valley, over rocks and boulders. At the first fork, turn to the right. Now the route becomes more difficult: you'll have to clamber over large, smooth rocks and boulders, and it can be quite dangerous if they are wet and slippery. Later the *torrente* passes through high and narrow clefts, between huge rocky cliffs. At the second fork, take the left-hand turning, and now the route becomes somewhat easier. Eventually we cross the main path, just below the houses of Mortitx (5h).

While it's always more enjoyable to return by a different route, it's more sensible to go back to Mortitx the way we came. The return is a bit faster past the point where the low walls meet: follow the rocky path marked with red paint (only easily seen from this direction), until you reach the colourful marker stone; here turn right for Mortitx (4h).

17 POLLENSA · THE TERNELLES VALLEY · EL CASTELL DEL REI · POLLENSA

Distance: 14km/8½mi; under 5h

Grade: easy to Ternelles; climb of 400m/1300ft on good track beyond

Equipment: stout shoes, sunhat, picnic, water; in winter, anorak and headscarf

How to get there: 🚌 to Pollensa; see also **STOP PRESS**, p168
Depart Palma at: 10.00, 13.30, 17.30, 19.15 weekdays; departures at 10.00, 16.30, 20.30 Sundays and holidays; journey time 1 hour
To return: 🚌 from Pollensa to Palma
Depart Pollensa: 07.30, 09.15, 14.15, 17.45 weekdays; departures at 08.15, 15.00, 19.00 Sundays and holidays; journey time 1 hour

Short walk: Pollensa to the Ternelles stream *and return* (A→B→A: 6km/3½mi; 2h). Easy, on good track; equipment as above

This easy walk through the beautiful oak-shaded valley of the Ternelles river leads you up to the bleak coastal mountains and to the ancient ruins of a thirteenth-century castle. The walk can be made at any time of the year, since

there's sufficient shade in the wooded valley – but put on your sunhat for the final stretch – a climb in full sun.

Leave the bus in the Calle Marques Destrull and start the walk: use the map to follow the main street, through the Plaza Mayor and the smaller plaza with a fountain surmounted by a metal cockerel (the 'Fuente del Gallo'). The Calle Montesión and the Calle de la Huerta will then lead you to the bridge over the Torrente de San Jordi.

For Walk 18, turn south from the bus stop, along the Calle Santo Domingo or Pollentia to find the K51.9 marker on the main PM220. Calvary Hill is also shown on the map (see page 34).

130

From here you can see the old Roman bridge over to the right (**20min**). Cross the main Lluc—Pollensa road (C710) carefully, and take the road straight ahead of you, signposted to Ternelles. This is a narrow tarmac country road, which winds its way through the various *possesiós* or *fincas*, through small cultivated areas and farm houses, populated with olive and fig trees. A dilapidated wooden signpost on the bend where the road turns right indicates the way. This area is called the 'Huerta de la Font' (the Fountain Market Gardens), and it's one of the most delightful country roads on Mallorca.

Following along, you will soon (**40min**) see a modern *canaleta* going under a small stone bridge, and, immediately beyond, round the corner, look up to see a most original balcony on an old house on your right — it's made from the large wooden screws taken from an old olive press. Continuing along, you'll have an old stone wall (which still carries water in a channel at the top) on your right. Ignore the path to the left, which is private property, and keep discovering the valley of evergreen oaks and the Torrente de Ternelles. At **50min** you'll pass some water deposits on the right — storage for Pollensa. Just past here, you can see the Serra de Cornavaca up right, where some neolithic village sites have been excavated. Looking down into the stream on the left, you'll spot the *canaleta* which used to carry water to Pollensa (and sometimes still flows).

Here you are now, in the valley, the Estret (Narrows) de Ternelles, where the road passes between the narrow rocky cliffs, just beyond which you can see the Roman aqueduct below the wall on your left.

At **55min** the large green gates of Ternelles confront you. Go through the small access gate to the right (the 'no entry' indication applies only to cars). You will now find a flat earthy track, which widens out a great deal just a bit further on and is shaded by large sturdy oaks. Notice the beautifully neat stone walls along here, just below the large house. After a minute or two the fountain of Ternelles peeps out at you from its hiding place amongst the trees on the right. Walk on through these beautiful shady glades, occasionally hearing the tinkling of sheep bells, until you come to a neat stone wall which protects a large cultivated area on the right. Ignore the small *camino forrestal* across the stream on your left, where there are stepping stones. This is one nice place to picnic and call a halt to the short walk. Or continue a bit further by passing through the green gates straight ahead (*not* the gates to the farm on the

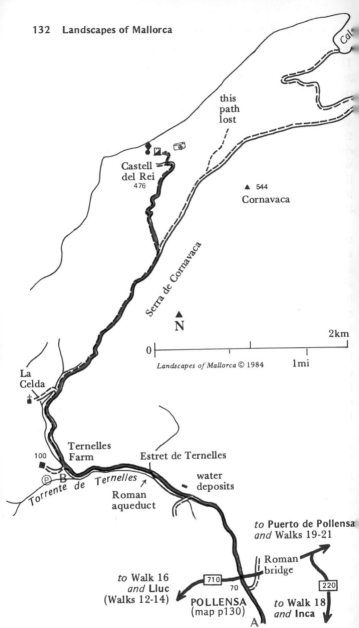

left). If they are locked, go through the wooden access gate
to the left, and continue along this pretty woodland walk,
perhaps picnicking just past the gates, to end the short walk.

From here onwards, you might scan the skies from time
to time, in the hope of sighting a black vulture. They are so
majestic, large and dark, gliding silently in circles over the

mountains, with a mighty wingspan of over three metres. These enormous birds take to remaining in one specific area, once having built their nest. We have seen them twice on this walk, so you might be lucky!

At **1h15min** go through more gates, over the bars which stop animals from wandering, and later take the signposted track up to the right (the way to the left leads to an old *ermita*, La Celda (The Cell). The route now leads on upwards, and you'll soon pass the remains of an old burnt limestone oven, to the right of the path. After a steady ascent, as you clear the trees, you will be able to see the large rocky clifftop in the distance.

The castle doesn't look very impressive yet, but wait and see! At under **2h** you'll come to a fork. Turn up left for the castle. (The continuing track leads on for some 5km down as far as the coast at Cala Castell.) From here it takes a good thirty minutes to reach the castle. The track is good, but uphill all the way and fairly steep. It comes to a dead end just below the ruins. About 50m (yds) before the track terminates, find the small stony path (not easily distinguishable at first) up the side of the slope. If you head straight for the bit of stone wall ruin that is separated from the castle itself, you should find it easy going. Just past here, the old broken steps will lead you through an impressive entrance into the precincts of this ancient fortress, an important island stronghold in Moorish times and later, after the Spanish conquest of the island. You'll be amazed at the size of it, and it's exciting to explore the different 'wings' — but do be careful of the steep drops to the sea in places. There is an old shelter here — unfortunately also in ruins — and an old well.

The views along this wild and rugged northern coastline are splendid. Cala Castell and Cala Estremer lie way below you, and the Serra del Cavall Bernat, just past Cala San Vicente, and the rocky Formentor cliffs can also be seen. There is something rather desolate about the bleak mountains along this uninhabited stretch of coastline, especially in winter. It must have been a lonely and chilly, windswept existence for the inhabitants of this stronghold, especially on a dark, stormy winter's night.

The walk back now is easy, pleasant and downhill. It should only take you just under a couple of hours to arrive back in Pollensa, where you should have time left to explore this enchanting little town with its quaint shops and narrow alleyways. The bus leaves from the stop in the Marques Destrull, shown on the town sketch map (p130).

18 PUIG DE MARIA (POLLENSA)

Distance: 3.5km/2mi; 1¼h

Grade: easy, but ascent is 270m/885ft

Equipment: stout shoes, sunhat, picnic, water

How to get there: See Walk 17, p130, for Pollensa bus details; ask to be put off at the Puig de María (pugj day Mah-**ree**-ah), on the PM220 just opposite the town of Pollensa

Short walk: as far up the *puig* as you like; there are good

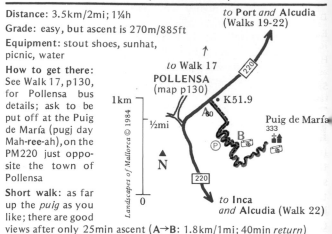

views after only 25min ascent (**A→B:** 1.8km/1mi; 40min *return*)

Opposite the town of Pollensa, a high, roundish mountain, the Puig de María, commands excellent views of the bays and the plain. **The walk starts** on the east side of the PM220, by the K51.9 marker (see town plan on page 130). The small country lane winds up through almond trees, towards the few small chalets built on the hillside. At the first bend, take the turning to the right, where blackberry bushes sprawl along the walls, and pass by the big, shady carob tree on the right. About five minutes along, take the bend up to the left (not straight on, where the road disappears), and continue winding up between the pretty houses with their flowering terraces. Now you can begin to admire the view of Pollensa, reposing peacefully in the protected valley, with its backcloth of high mountains etched against clear skies.

Soon the route is shaded by pine trees and tall oaks, making this ascent pleasantly cool, refreshed by sea breezes. At about **25min**, the path rounds the side of the mountain, from where you will have superb views of Alcudia and its bay. Past here, the centuries-old footpath is narrow and stony. A small grotto appears on a bend as the path climbs through palm bushes and tall pines bending in the wind. A small path leads off left at about **40min**. This narrow way leads to a small open area, where legend claims that the virgin appeared to three women. Five minutes later, you'll arrive at the top. Passing by the terraced area just below the church, go through the archway to the sanctuary, the Ermita de la Mare de Deu (see also pages 61 and 155), before you enjoy your picnic with its breathtaking views!

Distance: 6 km/3¾mi; under 2½h   **Grade:** easy climbs

Equipment: stout shoes, sunhat, picnic, water, anorak on cool days; long trousers, swimsuit, towel, suncream

How to get there: see bus timetables (p159) for Puerto de Pollensa; ask for 'Apartamentos Gommar'; return from Cala San Vicente by bus

Short walk: Hotel Don Pedro (**A**) as far as you like up Eagle Mountain (**B**); easy. Bus to Cala San Vicente; follow notes last paragraph

For some magnificent views of the rugged Formentor coastline, **start today's walk** at the Gommar apartments (map p136). Follow the narrow tarmac road opposite, and then the sandy track, as far as the old Finca Siller. (You may see loose guard dogs here; a stick is a wise precaution.) The track ends at the farm, but, just before the house, on the left, you will see a low brick wall between two hutches. Climb over the wall, to find yourself in the woods, where a quite easily seen trail leads on, towards the right. Go as far as the electricity pylons; then take the wider, stony path leading up left. In **25min** you'll come to a walled-in electricity plant on the hillside. Here turn sharp left in front of the walls, up the narrow, overgrown path through rocks and long grasses, marked at the outset by a large arrow made of loose stones on the ground. This winding path climbs to the low stone wall on the hillside, and follows up alongside it, coming out onto a track at about **35min.** Turn left again here, towards the white building belonging to the water board, and about 100m (yds) past the building another arrow of stones at ground level indicates a left turn through the low undergrowth, along the narrow path (the track leads on over the brow of the hill to some new houses). The path soon dips and rises again, through fire-scarred trees, until it widens out to pass lovely chalets and gardens on its way to the cove (**45min**). If you swim, *beware of the undertow!*

Now let's explore the other side of the *cala*. Take the steps up and over to the other (northern) beach. From here follow the main road past the Hotel Don Pedro, until you come to a large house with a landscaped garden (200m/yds). Turn right on the track beside the garden walls. At the fork, turn right again to pass through iron gates. From here follow the easy track for half an hour, until it ends by a cave at the right (**1½h**). *Experienced* walkers can scramble up over the pink, marble rock to the summit, but *beware of the two very deep holes* dropping down to the cave (see also Walk 21). From the Aguila (Eagle) mountain you'll have fabulous views of the *calas* and the cliff-tops of the Reial, where the ruins of Castell del Rei (Walk 17) tower over an indigo sea.

20 PUERTO DE POLLENSA · BOQUER VALLEY

Distance: 6 km/3¾ mi; 2¼ h   **Grade:** easy; gentle ascents/descents
Equipment/How to get there: as Walk 19; bus *into* Puerto de Pollensa
Short walk: Boquer Valley overlook and return (C→D→C: 3 km/
1¾ mi; 1¼ h); easy. Take sunhat, picnic, water; wear stout shoes

A very popular spot for bird-watchers, the long, wide Boquer valley reaches down to a lonely cove, where the elements venge their fury upon the rocks in winter, and the wind howls fiercely through, imprisoned by the jagged peaks of the Cavall Bernat to the north and the lower, bare mountains to the south that protect the Port of Pollensa.

Start out by heading northeast on the main road (signed to Formentor). Turn left through the iron gates onto the track to the Boquer farm, seen ahead on a ridge. Pass the house (**25min**) and go through the gate; then turn up right towards the old wooden gate. Beyond here lies the Boquer valley, silent and peaceful, save for the bleating of goats.

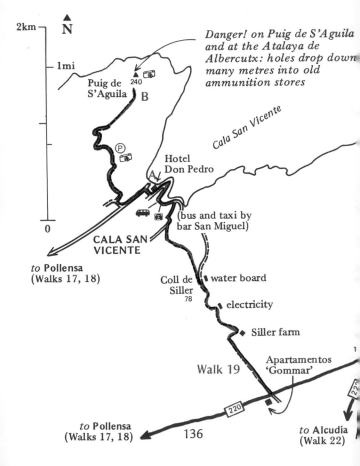

*Danger! on Puig de S'Aguila
and at the Atalaya de
Albercutx: holes drop down
many metres into old
ammunition stores*

2km

N

1mi

Puig de 240
S'Aguila
B

Cala San Vicente

P

Hotel
Don Pedro

A

(bus and taxi by
bar San Miguel)

0

CALA SAN
VICENTE

to **Pollensa**
(Walks 17, 18)

Coll de   water board
Siller
78   electricity

Siller farm

Walk 19

Apartamentos
'Gommar'

220

to **Pollensa**
(Walks 17, 18)   136

to **Alcudia**
(Walk 22)

Turn round to admire the views of the Bay of Pollensa and the plain, before you follow the way up through a 'wild-west ambush scene' of fallen rocks and boulders, through an opening in an old stone wall. Then cross open ground, with palm bushes and rosemary scrubs. Just ahead, you will see an ideal picnic spot: a grassy rise, shaded by a group of tall pines. End your short walk here (**D**); the views are very fine.

At **45min** pass an old well (dry in summer) and continue along the right-hand side of the valley — the path finding its way through gaps in the old stone walls. Soon you'll glimpse the deep blue sea, and the enormous rock of Es Colomer, just off the rocky Formentor coastline. At **1h** come to a second natural water fountain, trickling into a stone trough. From here, another ten minutes will get you onto the beach. If the sea is calm, you make like to swim in this stony cove. Perhaps you will be lucky enough to spot some migratory birds — or even a black vulture — on this outing!

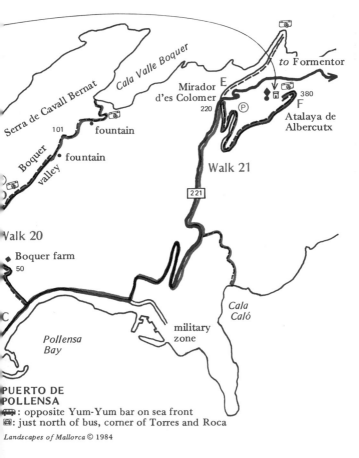

to Formentor

Cala Valle Boquer

Mirador
d'es Colomer
220

E

F
380

Atalaya de
Albercutx

Serra de Cavall Bernat

101

fountain

Boquer valley

fountain

Walk 21

221

Walk 20

Boquer farm
50

Cala
Caló

military
zone

C

Pollensa
Bay

**PUERTO DE
POLLENSA**
: opposite Yum-Yum bar on sea front
: just north of bus, corner of Torres and Roca

Landscapes of Mallorca © 1984

21 PUERTO DE POLLENSA · S'ATALAIA DE ALBERCUTX · CALA CALO

Distance: 10km/6mi; 3½h   **Grade:** easy, but many ups and downs!

Equipment/How to get there: as Walk 19; bus *into* Puerto de Pollensa
Taxi from Puerto de Pollensa to 'Mirador d'es Colomer'

Short walk: *mirador* parking place to Atalaya de Albercutx and
and return (E→F→E: 3km/1¾mi; 1¼h; fairly steep climb up a track;
take sunhat, picnic, water (headwear and warm clothing in winter).
Be sure to ask the driver to return for you (see 'Language hints', p157)

S 'Atalaia de Albercutx stands at 380m, overlooking the
incredibly beautiful bay of Formentor and its peninsula. **Our walk starts** at the steps to the *mirador* 'Es Colomer'
(map p137), where there's likely to be a crowd of tourists.
Follow the track opposite the steps to the *mirador*, beside
a low brick wall. You'll round the hill, to find the tiny cove
of El Caló and Formentor coming into view. At about **25
min**, you'll see the entrance to a long, dark tunnel cut into
the mountainside, on your left: this was built just after the
Spanish Civil War, during World War II, and was meant for
storing arms and ammunition. Five minutes later, past an
old brick water cistern, you'll see a small path leading off
over the brow of the hill towards a radio transmittor. If you
decide to investigate here, be *extremely careful!* There are
holes in the ground that drop right down into the tunnel!

The main route leads past the old army barracks (again
dating back to the Civil War). Go to the highest building
and find the path, at the right of the garage, that leads up
to the *atalaya*. Again — use care — there is only a low,
broken wall surrounding the top of the watchtower, and
sometimes the wind is fierce.

The half-hour descent to the PM221 is easy, although
stony; turn left and follow the road past the K4 marker, to
where a sandy track leads off left, just where the road bends
and is spanned by electricity wires (**1h45min**). Climb up
here, and pass by the side of a pylon, continuing straight
ahead; the narrow way will then descend the opposite side
of the hill. It's a rather narrow, overgrown and rocky path,
and there are places where you must *take care not to lose
your footing on the loose stones*. It takes about twenty
minutes to reach the beach, where you are guaranteed to
find peace and seclusion. The deep blue waters lap up on
the white pebbles, and the distant cries of seagulls carry on
the wind; no other sounds can be heard. Here, you can
picnic and watch the busy boatloads of tourists passing by.
But only swim if it's very calm; the beach drops off steeply,
and there is a strong undertow. From the beach it's just
over an hour back to the Port on the PM221.

22 ERMITA DE LA VICTORIA · PEÑA ROJA · ATALAYA DE ALCUDIA · PLAYA DE COLL BAIX · ALCUDIA

Distance: 17km/10¼mi; under 6h

Grade: Quite strenuous climbing during the first half of the walk; easy walking during the latter half; all paths are good

Equipment: stout shoes, sunhat, picnic, water, anorak

How to get there: 🚌 to Alcudia
Depart Palma 09.45; arrive Alcudia 10.45
Taxi (see village map p140) *from Alcudia to 'Ermita de la Victoria'*
To return: 🚌 from Alcudia *or* Puerto de Pollensa to Palma (see last paragraph of text on page 142)
Depart Alcudia 18.15; arrive Palma 19.30 daily *summer only*
Depart Puerto de Pollensa 17.30; arrive Palma 18.45 weekdays; departs Puerto de Pollensa 18.45 Sundays and holidays

Short walk: Ermita de la Victoria to Peña Roja *and return* (A→B→A: 3.5km/2mi; 1½h). Fairly strenuous climb of 400m/1300ft; equipment as above. Taxi to the Ermita and ask him to return for you in time for your bus (see timetables pp159-61 and 'Language hints' p157)

Turquoise, royal blue, pale and deep green — these are just some of the shades of the sea along the beautiful, rocky coastline on the Aucanada peninsula. Contrasting with the deep green of the pines, and the sandy-coloured cliffs, this is an artist's paradise of colour. The best time of year for this outing is early on in the year, on a clear sunny day when the cold air sparkles and visibility is good. Or in the springtime, when a pleasant sea breeze cools the effects of the Mallorcan sun.

Leave the bus in Alcudia and find a taxi to take you to 'Ermita de la Victoria', where **the walk begins**. The track you want starts behind the old *ermita*, opposite the car park. Follow the wide and comfortable track as it climbs (quite steeply), taking in all the wonders of the views and breathing deep lungfulls of pine-scented air. At **20min** the track takes a sharp turn to the right: just beyond, you will see the small narrow path leading up to the Peña Roja, signposted by ICONA. This delightful little route takes you alongside the mountain, rounding the cliffs, following the coastline right along the headland, as far as the old *atalaya*, from where there are magnificent views of the Bay of Pollensa and the Formentor headland — a delightful place to end your short walk with a picnic by the old stone refuge, once used by the *atalaya* watchmen. The beautiful Cape of Pines lies below you, surrounded by the many-hued coastal waters — a colourful picture postcard. Perhaps you'll make a ten-minute climb up to the actual watchtower on the rocky cliff behind the refuge, where you'll see the old cannon amidst the ruins.

139

Those making the long walk will return to the main track (1h30min) and continue along, rounding the Puig de Romany. A protective wooden fence ensures no feelings of vertigo as you climb towards the Atalaya de Alcudia on the now rocky path, looking out over the sea towards Menorca. In 2h walking you will attain the highest point in the walk, when you reach this *atalaya*. The splendid panorama from here is indescribably beautiful, and a good part of the island may be seen. The impressive Cordillera lies to the right, with the plain below. Then following round, find the landscapes of so many of our island walks: the *puigs* — Mayor, Massanella, Tomir; the headlands of Pollensa, the mountains of Artá. Below, near the beaches of Alcudia, the Albufera marshes glisten under the sun.

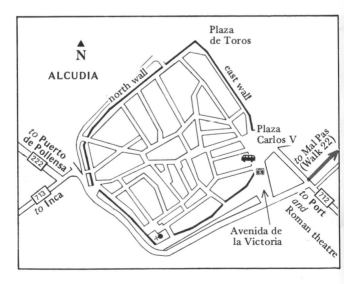

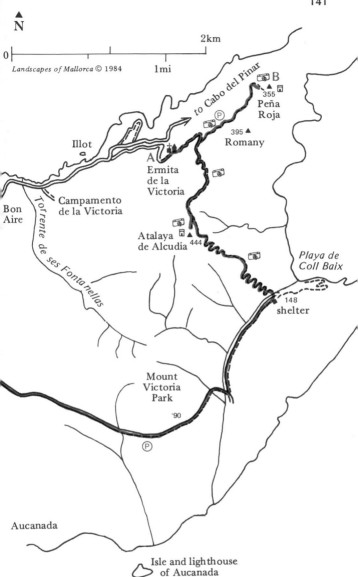

Returning from the *atalaya*, take the right-hand path, leading to the Playa de Coll Baix, a beautifully rugged, unspoilt beach between the cliffs. During the winding descent you'll see the small islet of Aucanada and its little lighthouse. Be sure to wear your sunhat here, at least until you reach the welcome shade of the pines at a lower level.

You'll have a splendid view of the *playa* far below from a high rocky pinnacle and, fifteen minutes later (3h), you come to an ICONA shelter — a welcome sight with its wooden tables and benches, and drinking fountain. This is an ideal spot for a picnic, under the shade of the trees, with the sound of the rollers breaking on the beach below.

As a picnic alternative, you could go right down to the beach, but there's little shade. It takes about fifteen minutes to reach the beach along this easy, narrow path, winding through the trees. Further down, the trees thin out, and the sparkling Caribbean-coloured waters swell in the small rocky cove. The sound of rollers breaking on the rocks can be quite deafening if the sea is agitated. Just before you get as far as the beach, the path is lost amongst the rocks. Some remains of wooden handrails help you along for a while, but the last lap involves clambering over the fallen rocks and boulders. Be careful if the sea is rough: large waves can cover these rocks, making them slippery and difficult to negotiate. However, there is no tide, so there is no danger of being cut off on the beach! But bathing in the sea is not to be recommended: there is a mighty undertow, and very strong undercurrents further out. In fact, from above the beach, you will see the sand swirling out for a good 200m or more.

Allow twenty minutes to come back up to the shelter. From here, follow the track straight ahead that leads on downwards through the pines. The way is wide and pleasant, with views of the sea from time to time, and a variety of birds singing. Keep always to the main track, which curves on down through the peaceful, pine-clad valley and quite soon you will have a view of the Aucanada lighthouse on your left.

One hour after leaving the shelter at Coll Baix (**4h45min**) you'll arrive at some double iron gates, which mark the end of the Mount Victoria Park. You will find yourself on a narrow tarmac country road which will lead you back to the Bodega del Sol bar at the crossroads, opposite the Bar Ca'n Tomeu, in about half an hour (**5h15min**).

From here it's another 2km, or about 45 minutes on foot to Alcudia. If you've shortened the long walk (perhaps by omitting the climb to Peña Roja, or the decent to the beach at Coll Baix), you may have time to walk into the village and catch the *summer* 18.15 bus (in winter, the departure is too early — 14.15). Alternatively, you can ask at the bar for a taxi to be called, to take you to Alcudia — or to Puerto de Pollensa, for the later bus departure.

23 BETLEM · ES CALO (ARTA)

Distance: 4.5km/2¾mi; 1¾h   **Grade:** easy

Equipment/How to get there: as Walk 24 (p144), but ask taxi driver to take you to (and collect you from) Betlem

Short walk: Betlem to the abandoned house and return (A→B→A: 2km/1¼mi; 40min; easy; stout shoes, sunhat, picnic, water)

An exhilarating stroll, characterised by the sound of rollers breaking below on the rocks and the tangy scent of pines. From the Colonia de San Pedro, continue in your transport along the tarmac road, as far as the new summer residential area of Betlem, its sparkling white houses reminiscent of Binibeca on Menorca. Here's where **the walk starts.**

About 100m (yds) beyond the last chalet, the tarmac road ends, and a stony track begins (leave your car 20m up this track, if you're driving). Then follow on foot through some stone gate-posts, and start to meander along the coast. You'll soon have beautiful views of the wide bay of Alcudia: Ca'n Picafort is visible, and further on round the bay, the holiday resort of Alcudia and the Aucanada peninsula — all with the rocky Formentor headland as a background.

The walk alternates between open stretches and pines. Not long after setting out, Mount Morey towers high above on our right (561m/2840ft) — the highest point on the Artá range. At about **20min**, you'll come to a small abandoned house on the right — a good place to end the short walk with a picnic. There's a patio round the back, from where a path leads up behind the house, into the mountains.

Continuing along the track, it takes about an hour to reach the small bay of Es Caló, where one or two fishing craft bob gently up and down on the sheltered waters, protected from the heavy swell of the sea by a jetty. Here, amongst the trees, there is a camping site and one or two rough fishermen's shelters; beyond, the track ends at a rocky headland. *(A difficult path leads from here to Cape Farruch — only for experts.)* On your return to Betlem, you'll leave behind busy cormorants gliding swiftly across the waters, looking for a catch.

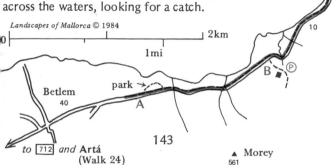

Landscapes of Mallorca © 1984

24 CALA MATZOCS · TORRE DE AUBARCA · PLAYA D'ES VERGER (ARTA)

Distance: 10km/6mi; under 3½h   **Grade:** easy ups and down

Equipment: stout shoes, sunhat, picnic, water, swimsuit, sun cream

How to get there: 🚌 to Artá (journey time 1½h)
Depart Palma 08.30 (Sun); dep 13.30 Mon—Sat; in *summer only*, als
dep Palma 10.00 Mon—Sat. *Taxi to Cala Estreta and return to Artá*
NB: The Artá taxi rank (Calle Son Servera, 24) is on the other side
of town from the bus stop (Avenida del Ferrocarril — C715).
Telephone for a taxi from the Café Parisien (Tel: 562202). See
'Language hints', p157, to ask the driver to collect you for the
return journey no later than 30 minutes before bus departure time
To return: 🚌 from Artá to Palma (journey time 1½h)
Departs Artá 14.10 daily all year and 17.35 Mon—Sat all year

Short walk: Cala Estreta to the Torre de Aubarca and return
(A→B→A: 2½km/1½mi; 1¼h); easy; equipment as above

The sea spray splashes over the bare rocks and sting
your cheeks, as you stroll over the headlands along the
rugged northern coastline of the Artá peninsula. Here there
are numerous sandy beaches, far enough away from civilisation to be deserted, even in summer — and the Isle of
Menorca can be seen floating on the horizon on a clear day
Yet there is a desolate air hanging over the mountains, a
strange sadness about the hillsides, ravaged by multiple fire:
which have left only the writhing skeletons of once-majestic
mountain pines.

The beauty of the coast more than makes up for the

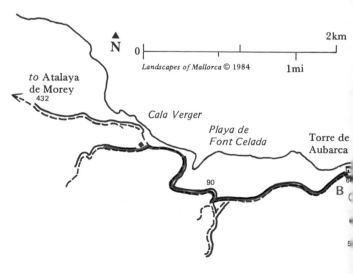

oneliness of the mountains, however, and this is an easy walk suitable for any time of the year (although by public transport only convenient in summer months). If the idea of spending a day on the beach 'far from the madding crowd' appeals to you, then this is the place to visit.

By car or taxi make for Cala Estreta (see notes in italics below — the road is not shown on most motoring maps). Here you'll see big open gates, the splendid entrance to an *urbanización* that was never built. Pass through, and keep to the left, turning left a few minutes later and driving down towards the sea. You'll see a sort of entrance gate on the right; here's where you leave your transport. The track we take begins just opposite, on the left-hand side of the road.

Start the walk along this track. You'll notice small palm bushes pushing up through the dry, sandy terrain. This is one of the three main areas on the island where they grow; you'll also see them in the Boquer valley and all around Pollensa, gradually disappearing in the mountains and then re-emerging in the south around Andraitx.

The track forks in six minutes; keep left and it will give way to a path, just past some heaps of stones on the right. Soon the Faralló de Aubarca, a large rock jutting out of the sea, is seen — and the ancient Aubarca tower on the headland.

Let's go down to the first beach, at Cala Matzocs. We cross this pretty, sandy cove to the opposite side, where we

Faralló de Aubarca

Cala Matzocs

The road to Cala Estreta is not shown on most motoring maps. Leave Artá on the Cala Ratjada road (C715). Turn left 500m past the town boundary. After a further 300m, turn right at the T junction north of the football stadium: this narrow tarmac road continues to Cala Estreta.

Cala Matzocs

beach

see a recess in the rocks (see sketch). The path continues up here and turns right round the rocky headland — but don't go *too* far right, where the flaking rock might be dangerous. We then climb a slope on the left (past a large rock with an 'A'), and continue along the coast. The path is somewhat lost here, but it is easy if you just head for the tower, which you should reach in under **40min.**

It is interesting to explore the *atalaya*, being careful as you climb the precarious steps up to the watchpoint at the top. Notice the perfectly constructed dome where one's faint whisper echoes mysteriously all around the walls! Up on the top rests an old rusty canon, bored with centuries of inactivity. There are some lovely views of the coastline as far as the Formentor headland, and of Menorca.

Now take the wide track that leads off directly in front of you, through still-surviving pines, and at **50min** pass through an old gate. At **1h10min** there are one or two forks in the track. Continue straight on and turn right a minute later where the track bends, following down towards the sea, with the salty tang of the wind. You'll soon arrive at the Playa de Font Celada (**1h25min**).

The track circles this beach and later rounds the rocky headland, keeping close to the coastline and passing by two solitary tamarind trees braving the sea spray on a windy day. Then we reach the Cala Verger and its *playa* (**1h40min**).

Now make your way up to the deserted house set back from the beach. Beyond here, a shady group of pines, and further down in the woods, some old tables and benches, make this a perfect spot for picnicking. However, if it isn't too hot, you will probably prefer to picnic on the beach, where your only companions will be the screeching seagulls and the busy comorants fishing for a tasty morsel.

It is possible to continue southwest along the track, past the house, where the white and twisted skeletons of the low pines bemoan their fate. Climb up onto the hillside past strawberry trees and low scrub bushes, as far as the old ruined hut on the *meseta*, where the track ends.

Or, if you are in an energetic mood, you can even continue west towards the mountain called Sa Torre, where the Atalaya de Morey looks out high over the sea. But this is a tiring scramble up about 400m (1500ft) — about 3h return from here.

25 CALA RATJADA · CALA GUYA · COLL DE MARINA · CALA MESQUIDA

Distance: 7km/4¼mi; 2½h **Grade:** easy ups and downs

Equipment: stout shoes, sunhat, picnic, water, swimwear, suncream

How to get there: 🚌 to Cala Ratjada (journey time 2h)
Depart Palma 08.30 Sundays; dep 13.30 Mon—Sat. In *summer only*, there is an additional Mon—Sat departure at 10.00
To return: 🚌 from Cala Ratjada to Palma (journey time 2h)
Departs 13.45 daily; also 17.05 Mon—Sat all year round

Short walk: Cala Ratjada to Coll de Marina (A→B→A: 4.5km/2¾mi; 1¾h *return*); easy climb. Equipment as above. May be combined with a scramble over the headland to the watchtower

A multitude of white sandy bays, bathed by turquoise lagoons, and bordered by deep green pine woods, awaits your discovery along the eastern coast of the island. Unfortunately, the groping tentacles of commercialism are also reaching into these paradisial hideaways, converting some of them into miniature concrete jungles, and such has been the sad fate of Cala Ratjada.

However, there is hope that the remaining untouched beaches will be preserved in their natural state, and so keep the ever-present threat of hotel construction at a distance.

Today's walk starts at the Plaza de los Pinos in Cala Ratjada, where we leave the bus. Walk east on the Calle Isaac Peral as far as the church; here turn left on the Calle Pascual Marques. This road leads right through to Cala Guya, reached in under **15min**.

Cala Guya is a beautiful, half-moon shaped bay, edged by sand dunes and bathed by a tranquil lagoon of pale blue and aquamarine waters, which has managed to retain some of its natural magic, in spite of the overflow of sun-seekers from neighbouring Cala Ratjada — although the beach here is sadly marred by large and ugly drinks kiosks in summer.

Let's go further afield. Walk right round the beach, to the northern end, past the 'sun-bed limit' signpost, towards the green garage doors in the trees. Go to the right of the garage doors, to find a small sandy track that continues ahead. (The track to the right leads out onto the small rocky headland of Es Guyó.)

Now we have a pleasant and easy hour's pine-shaded walk through the woods, over the Coll de Marina (145m/ 475ft). At **40min** pass by an old stone hut and go through an opening in the old stone wall. Ignore the small path to the right just beyond here, and other offshoots of the main track. When the track forks into two at **45min**, take the left fork, which leads up to the pass. A spot of red paint on a tree at **50min** indicates that you should continue on ahead

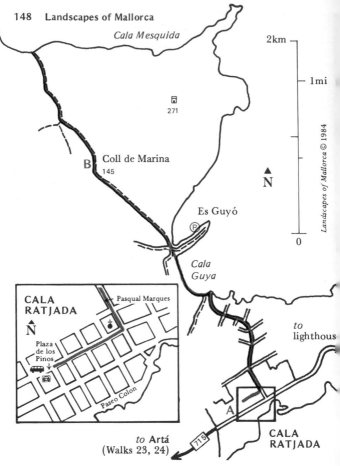

Cala Mesquida

2km

1mi

Landscapes of Mallorca © 1984

271

B Coll de Marina
145

▲
N

Es Guyó

Ⓟ

Cala Guya

0

CALA RATJADA

Pasqual Marques

▲
N

Plaza de los Pinos

Paseo Colon

to lighthouse

A

CALA RATJADA

to Artá
(Walks 23, 24)

715

ignoring the path to the left. Ten minutes later, pass by a low stone building in ruins. Soon the path begins to descend again towards the sea. Pass by a wide open space on the left, and at the fork, take the right-hand path, and then the left, following the way indicated by the stone arrows on the ground.

In **1h15min** you'll arrive at Cala Mesquida, where you can make your way down to the beach by going through the gap in the old broken wall, or explore over the rocky headlands of the Artá peninsula. Here, too, there are already about half a dozen new hotels straddled on the rocks high above the bay, but an idyllic air wafts on this elysian stretch of wide beach, which is never crowded, even in summer. The lonely surrounding hillsides, and the rugged headland where the *atalaya* still searches the horizon for any pirate ships, make other good picnic spots.

31

32

33

34

35

37

36

38

39

40

Atalayas

The *atalayas* are ancient watchtowers, built in the latter half of the sixteenth century, to guard against the frequent attacks of pirates and the ever-growing menace of invasion by the Turks.

More than thirty of these *atalayas* were in action in the year 1595, and much of the credit for their strategic siting is due to the magnificent work of Juan Binimelis — an astrologer, mathematician, doctor, priest and chronicler. His vast knowledge of the terrain, of topography, of artillery and of engineering made it possible to raise these stone outposts at the most suitable points. At the same time, other means of defence — such as La Torre in the Port of Alcudia and La Fortaleza de Albercutx — were in the planning stages.

From these high points of vigilance (called *talaias de foc* or 'fire towers' in Mallorquín), approaching sea-craft could be seen at a great distance, and fire and smoke signals were relayed across the island, warning of the danger. Once the enemy was sighted, the coastal inhabitants would take refuge, while the alerted naval forces would immediately move to the threatened areas.

You will encounter these watchtowers all round the island, and you'll visit several of them if you make any of our island walks. But even if you only see Mallorca from a car or coach, you'll surely visit the Talaia de Ses Animes, just south of Banyalbufar, now a superb *mirador*.

Let's consider just one interesting example of this network of watchtowers in action: A relay of signals between the Atalaya de Albercutx on the Formentor Peninsula (Walk 21), the Atalaya de Morey and the *atalaya* at Peña Roja on the Cape of Pines (Walk 22) and the Atalaya de Morey and Torre de Aubarca in the Artá mountains (Walk 24), more than adequately covered the only northern routes of entry to the island — the bays of Pollensa and Alcudia.

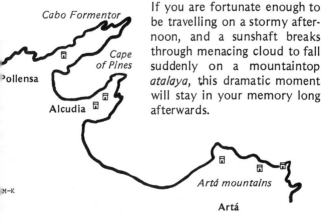

Cabo Formentor

Cape of Pines

Pollensa

Alcudia

Artá mountains

Artá

If you are fortunate enough to be travelling on a stormy afternoon, and a sunshaft breaks through menacing cloud to fall suddenly on a mountaintop *atalaya*, this dramatic moment will stay in your memory long afterwards.

M–K

Caça a coll

Thrushes are considered a great delicacy in Mallorca and the *caça a coll* (thrush-netting) is a tradition peculiar to the Balearic Islands.

The thrushes arrive in late autumn and winter from colder countries, and are especially fond of olives, but are themselves prey for larger birds, such as falcons and kestrels. Thus the thrushes fly only at dusk and early morning – between the tops of the tall oaks where they take refuge at night and the lower olive orchards. They tend to glide between the trees, and not above them, so as to protect themselves from the keen eyes of the bigger birds of prey.

The islanders noticed these habits and long ago devised a method of catching the birds. This consists of thinning out linear 'passages' between the trees and spanning a huge net held on two canes across the end of the passage. The *caçador* waits silently, hidden behind a bush, and when the birds fly down towards the netting, he quickly folds it over, thus capturing his unfortunate victims.

Many restaurants on Mallorca include this delicacy on their menus — the most popular dish perhaps being *tordo con col*, or roast thrushes wrapped in cooked cabbage leaves. It can be quite delicious, if you can force yourself to stop thinking of the poor little creature migrating happily to the sun, only to land up in the cooking pot!

Canaletes

These 'little canals' — irrigation channels — may still be seen around the island. Made of stone, they carry water from springs down the hillsides to irrigate crops. Today most of these delightful free-flowing water courses have been replaced by metal conduits, for reasons of sanitation and to prevent evaporation — a great loss for lovers of the landscape. The island's most famous *canaleta* is 7km long and runs between the Gorg Blau area and Mancor del Valle; its history is outlined on page 105. If you're lucky, you will be able to see a lovely *canaleta* in free flow if you make walk 17, in the Ternelles valley.

Casas de nieve

The *casas de nieve* (literally 'snow houses') are deep pits, only found on the highest part of the *sierra*. Here snow was stored to make ice before the advent of the refrigerator.

During the winter months, when heavy snow fell on the mountains, a group of men would set out for the peaks and fill these deep, stone-walled holes with snow, treading and packing it down hard. Once full, the pit was covered over with ashes or salt, and it remained frozen solid until the arrival of warmer weather. One man would stay behind, to tend the salt or ash covering, making repairs if necessary.

In summer, and at night, blocks of ice about fifty kilos (1 cwt) were loaded onto mules and taken down into the towns and villages, where they were used not only to make ice-creams and the like, but also for medicinal purposes. The so-called *oli de neu* (Mallorquín for 'snow-oil'), which was a mixture of ice and olive oil, was used to heal wounds and was reputed to stop bleeding.

There are many of these *casas de nieve* on the mountains of Massanella, Mayor, Teix and Tomir.

Ermitas

There are many *ermitas*, or sanctuaries, on Mallorca. Some of them are even today the homes of hermits who lead a lonely and solitary life. Dressed in long brown wool habits, their long white beards and shaven heads remind us of mediaeval times.

Although much early evidence of hermit life has been discovered on the island, Ramon Llull is accepted by the Mallorcans as being the founder of *eremetismo*. Born a few years after the invasion of Mallorca by Jaime I in 1229, Llull was the son of a Catalán who accompanied the king during his conquest. Ramon Llull himself then became the steward of the future king, Jaime II, while still in his teens. Later, he married Blanca de Picany, by whom he had two children. As he grew older, however, he found that his Latin passions could not be satisfied solely by his wife, and he turned to other *amantes* in search of further pleasure and deeper fulfillment.

At about the age of thirty, he experienced a sudden conviction of his sins and turned to strict penitence — making pilgrimages to the sanctuaries of Santiago de Compostela and Montserrat. Back on Mallorca, in 1275 he went to Randa, living in a small grotto on the hillside. Later, he founded a missionary school in Valldemossa, where oriental languages were taught to friars who would later travel in Asia and Africa to convert the followers of Islam.

Ramon Llull was martyred in North Africa in 1315, stoned to death by Saracens. His remains were brought back to Mallorca by a group of Genovese merchants, and his relics were placed in the Church of San Francisco in Palma.

A typical day in the life of a hermit starts at 01.00, when he rises for the first prayers of the day. A second call to prayer comes at 06.00, followed by breakfast and manual labour assigned by the superior. After the main meal is eaten at 12.30, the afternoon and evening are spent in prayer, self-examination, meditation and further labour. Lights are out at 21.00, and each hermit retires to his cell where he rests until, at 01.00, the day repeats itself. A love of the solitary life is a must for all would-be hermits!

The governing superior resides at the Sanctuary of San Salvador, near Felanitx (Tour 9), and is elected every six years by the hermits themselves. Novices begin their trial periods at the Ermita de Betlem near Artá (Tour 6).

Of special interest to lovers of the countryside (and walkers in particular) is the opportunity to stay overnight at various sanctuaries scattered around the island. The simple accommodation is spotless, and owing to the remote position of the *ermitas* on their hilltops, the overviews are always superb. See also page 61, 'Where to Stay'.

H ornos de calç

You'll see the remains of many of these ovens (*hornos*) around Mallorca. They were used to produce lime (*calç*) for whitening the interiors of houses, or to be mixed with fine gravel for use in building.

The work was carried out by three men usually, working day and night for anything between nine and fifteen days. A great amount of heat was necessary to produce the reaction: $CaCO_3 \overset{\Delta}{\to} CaO + CO_2$, and in these ovens an enormous quantity of wood was burned to obtain the heat required. Normally, the thinner logs which were not suitable for the charcoal industry (see *sitjas* below) were used, and any amount up to two tons could be burnt during one 'cooking'! Special stones, *piedra viva*, were used, and were usually found on the surrounding hillsides. A normal-sized oven would produce between a hundred and a hundred and fifty tons of burnt lime in one session.

S itjas

Circular earth mounds, ringed with stones and covered with moss — *sitjas* — are the only remains today of the old charcoal industry. In summer months the charcoal makers lived with their families in the oak woods on the mountainsides. The sturdiest logs from the holm oak were used, and the fires burned round the clock — producing about one and a half tons of charcoal in a week — but the work was poorly paid. Sometimes the remains of a stone hut dwelling are to be found near the *sitjas* (see Picnic 12).

Spanish and Mallorquín

While Spanish is the official language of Mallorca, most of the islanders speak Mallorquín amongst themselves. And the island, like many other regions around the world, has an active minority of citizens who would prefer to re-establish Mallorquín as the official language. This linguistic 'tug-of-war' manifests itself in many ways.

You will notice that spellings of place names vary between maps and signposts — for example 'Andraitx' and 'Andratx'. Similarly, both the Spanish form La Calobra and the Mallorquín Sa Calobra are seen.

Those of us who live on Mallorca use both languages interchangeably — hardly noticing the discrepancies that are so obvious to confused visitors. Rather than use either Spanish or Mallorquín in this book, I have adopted the spellings in most common usage on the island today and have tried to be consistent.

Hints for walkers and picnickers

In the tourist centres you'll find that almost everyone speaks at least a little English. But once out in the country-side, a few words of Spanish will be helpful, especially if you lose your way.

Here's an — almost — foolproof way to communicate in Spanish. First, memorise the few short key questions and their possible answers, given on the next page. Then, when you have your 'mini-speech' memorised, always ask the many questions you can concoct from it **in such a way that you get a 'sí' (yes) or 'no' answer.** Never ask an open-ended question such as 'Where is the main road?' You won't understand the answer — especially as it's likely to be given in Mallorquín! Instead, ask the question and then *suggest the most likely answer yourself.* For instance: 'Good day, sir. Please — where is the road to Lluc? *Is it straight ahead?'* Now, unless you get a '*sí*', try: '*Is it to the left?*' If you go through the list of answers to your own question, you will eventually get a '*sí*' response — probably with a vigorous nod of the head — and this is just that bit more reassuring than relying solely on sign language.

An inexpensive phrase book, such as one of those published by Collins, Berlitz, or Penguin, is a very valuable aid, from which you may choose other 'key' phrases and answers.

Following are three of the most likely situations in which you may have to practice some Spanish. The dots (...) show where you will fill in the name of your destination. The correct pronunciation of place names will be found in the index, on pages 162-168.

■ Asking the way

The key questions

English	Spanish	pronounced as
Good day,	Buenos días,	Boo-eh-nas dee-ahs,
sir (madam, miss).	señor (señora, señorita).	sen-yor (sen-yor-ah, sen-yor-ee-tah).
Please —	Por favor —	Poor fah-vor —
where is	dónde está	dohn-day es-tah
the road to ... ?	la carretera a ... ?	lah cah-reh-teh-rah ah ...?
the footpath to ... ?	la senda de ... ?	lah sen-dah day ...?
the way to ... ?	el camino a ... ?	el cah-mee-noh ah ...?
the bus stop?	la parada de autobus?	lah pah-rah-dah day ow-toh-boos?
Many thanks.	Muchas gracias.	Moo-chas gra-thee-as.

Possible answers

English	Spanish	pronounced as
here	aquí	ah-kee
straight ahead	todo recto	toh-doh rec-toh
behind	detrás	day-tras
to the right	a la derecha	ah lah day-reh-chah
to the left	a la izquierda	ah lah eeth-kee-er-dah
above	arriba	ah-ree-bah
below	abajo	ah-bah-hoh

■ Asking a taxi driver to return for you

English	Spanish	pronounced as
Please —	Por favor	Poor fah-vor
take us to ...	llévanos a ...	l-yay-vah-nos ah ...
and return	y volver	ee vol-vair
for us at ...	para nosotros a ...	pah-rah nos-oh-tros ah ...

(Instead of memorising hours of the day, simply point out the time when you wish him to return on your watch, and get his agreement.)

■ Meeting a landowner who denies you access

See notes on page 59 about right of way. If you believe that you have right of way, you might ask:

English	Spanish	pronounced as
We are going to ...	Nos vamos a ...	Nos vah-mos ah ...
If this way	Si este camino	See es-tay cah-mee-noh
is private,	es privado,	es pree-vah-doh,
please —	por favor —	poor fah-vor —
show us	muéstranos	moo-es-trah-nos
the way.	el camino.	el cah-mee-noh.
Many thanks.	Muchas gracias.	Moo-chas grath-ee-as.

■ Once in a while you may meet people who do not speak Spanish. Greet them in Mallorquín and then pronounce *very carefully* the name of the place you are looking for (see Index for pronunciation of landmarks in this book). The Mallorquín for 'Good morning' is *Bon día* (**Bone** dee-ah); 'Good afternoon' is *Bonas tardas* (**Bone**-ahs **tar**-dahs).

TRANSPORT TIMETABLES

Timetables are given on pages 160-161 for all the transport used to make the walks and picnics in this book. Use the alphabetical list of destinations below to find the appropriate timetable (note that 'Bus 1' means bus *timetable* 1 — not an actual bus number). Also included in the list below are some other departure times which you might find useful. Please remember that **changes to schedules are frequent.** Do not rely **solely** on these timetables, but get an up-to-date list from the Tourist Office or a tourist information kiosk near to your hotel. Also remember that while 'summer' generally means 1 May — 30 September, these dates are flexible — depending on weather conditions and how many tourists are about! It always pays to ask your hotel porter to 'phone to the transport company — or to go there yourself — to check the validity of whichever timetables you use — those in this book or even the ones from the Tourist Office! If you're staying outside Palma, enquire at your hotel to see if there are any useful local bus services in the area.

DESTINATION	departs from Palma			departs for Palma		
Alaró	see Train 1 (p161)					
Alcudia	see Bus 4 (p160)					
Andraitx	see Bus 5 (p160) and Bus 8 (p161)					
Artá	see Bus 1 (p160)					
Banyalbufar□	10.00			17.50*	18.35†	
Bunyola	see Train 2 (p161)					
Caimari	see Bus 3 (p160)					
Cala Bona	10.00	13.30	17.15	07.00	08.45	15.15
Cala d'Or	09.30	14.45	19.30	07.15	12.15	17.00
Cala Ratjada	see Bus 1 (p160)					
Cala San Vicente○	10.00	13.30		13.45	18.00	
Calas de Mallorca	10.00	17.15		07.45	09.15	15.00
Campanet	09.00†	12.45*		14.45*	17.00†	19.00*
Ca'n Picafort	09.45	13.30	18.15	07.40	09.00	16.00
Colonia San Jordi	19.30			07.50		
Deiá	see Bus 7 (p161)					
Esporles	see Bus 2 (p160)					
Estellenchs□	10.00			17.30*	18.15†	
Felanitx	09.30	13.00	16.00	08.00	14.00	17.45
Inca	see Bus 3, Bus 4, Bus 6 (p160) and Train 1 (p161)					
La Puebla	13.30	18.15		08.00	14.45	
Manacor	see Bus 1 (p160)					
Moscari	09.15	11.30	13.00	17.30	18.45	19.30
Muró	13.30	18.15		08.00	14.45	
Paguera	see Bus 5 (p160)					
Petra	09.30	13.00	16.30	07.30	14.25	17.50
Pollensa	see Bus 6 (p160) and **STOP PRESS** (p168)					
Porto Cristo	10.00	13.30	17.15	09.40	14.15	17.30
Porto Petro	14.45			16.30		
Puerto de Alcudia	see Bus 4 (p160)					
Puerto de Andraitx	see Bus 5 (p160)					
Puerto de Pollensa	see Bus 6 (p160) and **STOP PRESS** (p168)					
Puerto de Soller	see Bus 7 and Tram (p161); also **STOP PRESS** (p168)					
San Telmo	see Bus 8 (p161)					
Santa Eugenia	see Bus 9 (p161)					
Santa María	see Bus 6 (p160), Bus 9 and Train 1 (p161)					
Santanyí	09.30	14.45	19.30	07.50	12.50	17.30
Selva (see also Bus 3)	09.15	11.30	13.00	17.40	18.55	19.40
Ses Salines	09.30	14.45	19.30	07.45	13.05	17.40
Soller	see Train 2 and Tram (p161); also **STOP PRESS** (p168)					
Valldemossa	see Bus 7 (p161)					

□ summer only
*does not run on Sundays/holidays
†Sundays/holidays only
○also departures from Puerto de Pollensa

BUS 1
Palma — Manacor — Artá — Cala Ratjada

	Monday–Saturday				Sundays/holidays
Palma	10.00◻	13.30	17.15	19.45	08.30
Manacor	10.50◻	14.20	18.05	20.35	09.20
Artá	11.30◻	15.00	18.45	21.15	10.00
Cala Ratjada	12.00◻	15.30	19.15	21.45	10.30
Cala Ratjada	07.30	13.45	17.05		13.45
Artá	08.00	14.10	17.35		14.10
Manacor	08.40	14.55	18.15		14.55
Palma	09.30	15.45	19.05		15.45

BUS 2
Palma — Esporles

WINTER (1 October – 30 May)
Monday – Friday

Palma	07.25	12.00	13.15	16.30	18.15	19.30
Esporles	07.55	12.30	13.45	17.00	18.45	20.00
Esporles	07.00	07.55	09.10	14.45	18.40	
Palma	07.30	08.25	09.40	15.15	19.10	

Saturdays | Sundays/holidays

Palma	09.00	13.00	15.30	19.30	10.00	15.30	19.30
Esporles	09.30	13.30	14.00	20.00	10.30	16.00	20.00
Esporles	08.20	09.30	15.00	17.30	08.30	15.00	18.30
Palma	08.50	10.00	15.30	18.00	09.00	15.30	19.00

SUMMER (1 June – 30 September)
Monday – Saturday

Palma	10.00	12.00	14.00	16.00	19.30	20.30
Esporles	10.30	12.30	14.30	16.30	20.00	21.00
Esporles	07.45	09.10	15.30	18.30		
Palma	08.15	09.40	16.00	19.00		

Sundays and holidays

Palma	10.00	16.00	20.00
Esporles	10.30	16.30	20.30
Esporles	09.10	15.30	19.15
Palma	09.40	16.00	19.45

BUS 3
Inca — Selva — Caimari — Lluc
(connects with train from Palma)

Inca	09.45	17.00	Lluc	11.00	18.00
Selva	09.55	17.10	Caimari	11.15	18.15
Caimari	10.05	17.15	Selva	11.20	18.20
Lluc	10.20	17.35	Inca	11.30	18.30

BUS 4
Palma — Inca — Alcudia — Puerto de Alcudia

Palma	09.45	12.00	13.30	18.00	19.00◻
Inca	10.00	12.15	13.45	18.15	19.15◻
Alcudia	10.45	13.00	14.30	19.00	20.00◻
Puerto de Alcudia	11.00	13.15	14.45	19.15	20.15◻
Puerto de Alcudia	07.15	09.15	11.15	14.15	18.15◻
Alcudia	07.30	09.30	11.30	14.30	18.30◻
Inca	07.55	09.55	11.55	14.55	18.55◻
Palma	08.30	10.30	12.30	15.30	19.30◻

BUS 5
Palma — Paguera — Andraitx — Puerto de Andraitx

Frequent departures, too numerous to schedule. Approximate journey times as follows: Palma — Paguera 40min; Paguera — Andraitx 20min; Andraitx — Puerto de Andraitx 15min
WINTER: buses depart Palma daily at 07.10 and every 45min thereafter until 19.30; depart Puerto de Andraitx 07.15 and every 45 minutes thereafter until 19.30
SUMMER: more frequent buses, with departures at both ends of the route at the following times

07.00	07.35	08.10	08.45	09.30	09.55	10.30	11.05
11.40	12.15	12.50	13.25	14.00	14.35	15.10	15.35
16.20	16.55	17.30	18.05	18.40	19.15	20.00	

BUS 6
Palma — Santa María — Inca — Pollensa — Puerto de Pollensa

	Monday–Saturday				Sundays/holidays		
Palma	10.00	13.30	17.30	19.15	10.00	16.30	20.30
Santa María	10.20	13.50	17.50	19.35	10.20	16.50	20.50
Inca	10.40	14.10	18.10	19.55	10.40	17.10	21.10
Pollensa	11.00	14.30	18.30	20.15	11.00	17.30	21.30
Pto Pollensa	11.15	14.45	18.45	20.30	11.15	17.45	21.45
Pto Pollensa	07.15	09.00	14.00	17.30	08.00	14.45	18.45
Pollensa	07.30	09.15	14.15	17.45	08.15	15.00	19.00
Inca	07.50	09.35	14.35	18.05	08.35	15.20	19.20
Santa María	08.10	09.55	14.55	18.25	08.55	15.40	19.40
Palma	08.30	10.15	15.15	18.45	09.15	16.00	20.00

NB: All transport is daily unless otherwise coded

BUS 7

Palma — Valldemossa — Deía — Puerto de Soller

WINTER (1 October – 30 March)				
Palma	10.00	12.00*	15.00	19.00
Valldemossa	10.30	12.30*	15.30	19.30
Deía	10.45	12.45*	15.45	19.45
Pto Soller	11.15	13.15*	16.15	20.15
Pto Soller	07.30	15.00	17.30	
Deía	08.00	15.30	18.00	
Valldemossa	08.30	16.00	18.30	
Palma	09.00	16.30	19.00	

SUMMER (1 April – 30 September)					
Palma	07.45	10.00	12.00*	16.30	20.00
Valldemossa	08.15	10.30	12.30*	17.00	20.30
Deía	08.30	10.45	12.45*	17.15	20.45
Pto Soller	09.00	11.15	13.15*	17.45	21.15
Pto Soller	07.00	09.30	14.30	16.00*	18.30
Deía	07.30	10.00	15.00	16.30*	19.00
Valldemossa	08.00	10.30	15.30	17.00*	19.30
Palma	08.30	11.00	16.00	17.30*	20.00

BUS 8

Palma — Andraitx — San Telmo

Palma	09.00†		San Telmo	17.15†
Andraitx	10.00†		Andraitx	17.45†
San Telmo	10.30†		Palma	18.45†

BUS 9

Palma — Santa María — Santa Eugenia

	Monday–Saturday			Sun/holidays	
Palma	13.30	19.00		09.00	19.00
Santa María	13.50	19.20		09.20	19.20
Santa Eugenia	14.05	19.35		09.35	19.35
Santa Eugenia	07.00	08.00	15.15	08.00	18.00
Santa María	07.10	08.10	15.25	08.10	18.10
Palma	07.35	08.35	15.50	08.35	18.35

TRAINS

TRAIN 1

Palma — Santa María — Alaró y Consell — Inca

Palma	06.00	and every hour until	21.00
Santa María	06.15		21.15
Alaró y Consell	06.25		21.25
Inca	06.35		21.35
Inca	06.00	and every hour until	21.00
Alaró y Consell	06.10		21.10
Santa María	06.20		21.20
Palma	06.35		21.35

TRAIN 2

Palma — Bunyola — Soller

Palma	08.00	10.40	13.00	15.15	19.45	22.00†
Bunyola	08.26	11.08	13.26	15.40	20.10	22.25†
Soller	09.00	11.45	14.00	16.15	20.45	23.00†
Soller	06.45	09.15	11.50	14.10	18.20	21.00†
Bunyola	07.15	09.45	12.15	14.35	18.45	21.25†
Palma	07.45	10.15	12.50	15.10	19.20	22.00†

TRAM

Soller — Puerto de Soller

Departures from Soller							
05.55	07.00	08.00	09.00	10.00	11.00	11.30	12.00
12.30	13.00	14.00	15.00	16.00	16.30	17.00	17.30
17.55	19.00	20.00	20.45				

Departures from Puerto de Soller							
06.20	07.30	08.25	09.30	10.30	11.30	12.00	12.30
13.00	13.25	14.30	15.30	16.30	17.00	17.30	17.55
18.30	19.30	20.20	21.10				

BOAT

Puerto de Soller — La Calobra

Pto Soller	10.30	11.30	15.00	*Schedule depends*
La Calobra	11.20	12.20	15.50	*on weather. Boat*
La Calobra	14.00	15.00	17.00	*generally runs*
Pto Soller	14.50	15.50	17.50	*May–September*

□ summer only
* does not run Sundays/holidays
† Sundays/holidays only

Index

Geographical names only are included here; for non-geographical entries, see Contents, page 3. All indexing is in Spanish and follows the standard convention of indexing under the article: thus 'La Calobra' will be found under 'L', not 'C'. To save space, entries have been grouped together where possible, so, for instance, to find 'Campanet Caves', look under 'Caves': a cross-reference directs you to 'Cuevas'. Other headings used are: Atalaya (watchtower, tower), Cabo (cape), Cala (cove or bay), Castell (castle), Coll (mountain pass), Ermita (hermitage), Finca (farm), Font (spring), Isla (island), Mirador (viewpoint), Playa (beach), Puig (mountain), Torre (tower), and Torrente (stream). A page number in italic type indicates a map reference, often in addition to a text reference.

Glossary

Below are translations of the less-familiar Spanish and Mallorquín terms used in this book:

atalaya — watchtower
caça a coll — thrush-netting
caçador — hunter
camino — road, way
ca'n — contraction of the Mallorquín 'casa d'en' — 'house of'
canaleta — irrigation channel
carrer — street (Mallorquín)
carretera — highway
casa de nieve — snow pit
coll — pass
coll de caçar — 'shooting pass'; place for thrush-netting
comedero — feeding ground
cordillera — mountain range
coto privado de caça — private hunting ground
embalse — reservoir
ermita — hermitage

finca — farm
font — fountain, spring
fronton — pelota court
horno de calç — lime oven
parada — bus stop
pla — plain, tableland
planicie — plain, tableland
puig — mountain
rama — branch
romería — pilgrimage
senda — footpath, trail
serra — mountain range (Mallorquín)
sierra — mountain range (Spanish)
sitja — fireplace
son — 'estate of' (Mallorquín)
talayots — prehistoric stones
torrente — torrent or stream; Mallorca has *no* rivers

*see pages 153-156 for more details

STOP PRESS

The most important bus service for walkers is, without doubt, the one which runs from Soller (and its port) to the Port of Pollensa. At the time of writing, the service is less than ideal: in winter it runs only on weekends; in summer it is a daily service. However, there is only one bus a day, leaving Soller at 09.00 and returning from Puerto de Pollensa at 17.00. Hopefully this book will encourage more people to walk in the mountains, thereby encouraging a more ample bus service. Until a morning bus from Pollensa is introduced, this is *not* a good centre from which to make mountain walks. But Lluc is quite well placed for Walks 13, 14, 16, 17-21. Otherwise, Soller and Puerto de Soller become, along with Palma, the best overnight centres for walkers. The current timetable is

Soller	09.00	Pto Pollensa	17.00	*This service is*	
Pto Soller	09.30	C San Vicente	17.10	*daily in summer*	
Ses Barques	09.45	Pollensa	17.20	*(approximately*	
Army base	10.05	Lluc	18.00	*Easter until end*	
Escorca	10.20	Escorca	18.20	*September) and*	
Lluc	10.35	Army base	18.35	*weekends only*	
Pollensa	11.20	Ses Barques	18.50	*in winter.*	
Cala S Vicente	11.30	Pto Soller	19.10		
Pto Pollensa	11.45	Soller	19.25		